D0121768

Literary Criticism

Literary Criticism

A Practical Guide for Students

Malcolm Hicks

Staff Tutor in Literature
Department of Extra-Mural Studies
University of Manchester

and

Bill Hutchings

Lecturer in English Literature
Department of English Language and Literature
University of Manchester

Edward Arnold
A member of the Hodder Headline Group
LONDON   NEW YORK   MELBOURNE   AUCKLAND

Edward Arnold is a division of Hodder Headline PLC
338 Euston Road, London NW1 3BH

First published in the United Kingdom 1989

8   7   6   5   4
99 98 97 96 95 94

Distributed in the USA by Routledge, Chapman and Hall, Inc.
29 West 35th Street, New York, NY 10001

British Library Cataloguing in Publication Data
Hicks, Malcolm
Literary criticism: a student's guide.
1. Literature. Criticism
I. Title   II. Hutchings, Bill
801'.95

ISBN 0-7131-6582-0

Typeset by Colset Private Ltd, Singapore
Printed and bound in the United Kingdom by
Athenæum Press Ltd, Gateshead, Tyne and Wear

Contents

Preface

In designing this book for students of literature, our purposes are interrelated and threefold: first and foremost, to develop a sound appreciation of literature generally; secondly, to help students improve their performance in examinations and coursework, particularly those which present unseen passages for critical commentary; lastly, to provide an introduction to the broader spectrum of literary studies in higher education.

At its best, the process of literary criticism is one of continuing evolution and careful reappraisal of existing principles. So, while we fully recognize within these pages that the basic skills which you are required to develop actually derive from what has now become a traditional approach to criticism, our aim is also to help you to a more distinctive and satisfying achievement by giving you some awareness of the assumptions which underlie what you are doing and the new approaches to literature which have proliferated in recent years. These approaches have gained wider and wider currency and, surprising though it may seem, it could well be that such otherwise formidable 'isms' as post-structuralism, feminism, and their like, are already implicitly reflected in your own reading responses and group discussions. Our book should help to clarify and extend your thinking about the works you read.

The book begins with an approachable and wide-ranging guide to theory, followed by an extensive section of useful practical hints on answering examination questions. Since there is no confidence to be gained from those who do not, or cannot, practise what they preach, the middle section of the book is taken up with our analyses of literary examples, illustrative of those basic skills and issues discussed in the first part. We have taken the view that all writing is literature, involving the orchestration of language to reveal ideas, and that literary criticism can be profitably exercised on all types of text. So you will find examples on a broad range of subjects drawn not only from poetry, fictional prose and drama, but also from historical writing, the essay and journals. In the interests of comprehensiveness, these range from the sixteenth to the twentieth centuries. Exercises in unseen literary appreciation sometimes provide authors' names and titles of works from which the passages are taken, but we have decided to list our sources separately at the back of the book for you to consult when you choose. This is because the revealing of the writer's name and work seems to us a mixed blessing. Any information, no matter how limited, rightly encourages the notion that books do not somehow drop from the skies. On the other hand, if the information means something to you, you could be tempted beyond the immediate task in hand. Equally, if it means nothing, you could well be unsettled in an environment which calls upon all the coolness you can muster. Ideas should not be imposed as a result of any assumptions you might have about the author or work named, but generated from the passage in front of you.

Finally, in the closing part of the book we have sought to anticipate remaining uncertainties by offering answers to the questions that have most frequently arisen in the course of our discussions with large numbers of students. We know that students are understandably irritated by what they consider to be irrelevancies; that in the real world it is examination success which is all-important. Without wishing to encourage any kind of philistinism, we have sympathetically taken this to heart. In complementing the work of teachers and lecturers, we wish to equip our readers with the skills needed to respond to, and write perceptively about, the examples which they will confront in class and examination. These skills, we believe, will also help students to tackle their set texts, develop their wider reading, and advance their love of literature.

Part I
Theory and Practice of Criticism

(i) Propositions

The way in which people write brings its own assumptions and implications, and this is as true of the book you are reading as it is of any other. In our presentation of examples in Part II, we are assuming the validity of a certain type of criticism: that of a practical, or technical, kind capable of coming up with substantial objective observations even though each passage is divorced from its contexts. These include the rest of the work, the other works of the author and of his or her contemporaries, and that seemingly limitless field which we can both confine and define under the phrase 'the social and historical milieu'. Practical criticism of this kind remains the foundation of reading, and your development of the techniques it involves will help you in all areas of your literary studies. But it would be short-sighted not to take into account the new approaches to reading a text which have multiplied in recent years. These are in the process of questioning and qualifying the ideas which inform practical criticism, both as a challenge to, and development of, the basic reading process. In section (iii) of this part we introduce you to the most important of these new methods.

Offering passages in isolation is artificial. All literature has its context; but when we pause to consider just where we might fix the limits of time and place we come to find, no matter how comprehensive we strive to be, that boundaries are incapable of being determined. How much time, for example, would we need to devote to an investigation of the social and political world of Shakespeare's history plays to feel confident that we had the knowledge necessary for a definitive interpretation? It is important for you to preserve a careful balance between demonstrating the practical literary skills you have acquired on the details of set passages or texts and indicating your ability to discuss such wider matters as are prompted by them. It is all too easy to make over-confident generalizations for which neither your reading nor writing can provide a basis, yet it might be some comfort for you to know that even academics are not always blameless in this respect. It has often been the case that we have read and heard (and, in our weaker moments, been tempted into ourselves) casual remarks which would embarrass, say, the more scholarly social or economic historian. Perhaps the experienced critic is capable of the occasional broad observation, but you must be wary of those catch-all definitions which begin 'In the Renaissance . . .' or 'The nineteenth century was a time of . . .'. On the other hand, do try on the well-judged occasion to see the 'wood' from your exploration of the 'trees' which compose it.

(ii) Analysis and evaluation

Theory is implicit in any practice. Any syllabus involves choice, and selection is inevitably based upon principles, whether acknowledged or not. It is generally agreed that a knowledge of theory is essential to a full understanding of what we are doing when we engage with literature at any level. Practical criticism itself reflects theoretical assumptions, as a glance at its history shows. A useful point of origin to focus upon occurred in the 1920s when Professor I. A. Richards presented his Cambridge students with unattributed poems for their appraisal. He was shocked by what he considered to be the arbitrariness, or lawlessness, of their responses, contradicting the established reputations of the writers he had chosen. Reading literature had by then achieved the status of a discipline worthy of being studied at university, and there was a need to advance beyond vague, impressionistic responses and evolve fixed standards by which students' reactions could be judged.

Notice that the proponents of this new rigour believed that evaluations could indeed be made and justified. These were to be realized through intense scrutiny of individual texts, or passages from texts, paying attention to the categories students are still expected to examine in literary appreciation papers and assignments. This certainly testifies to the historical versatility of practical criticism, the analytical format of which embodies the desire to be scientific. But exercises in practical criticism often call for a response to questions such as 'how effectively does the passage . . .?' which are judicial and evaluative, although meant to derive from the application of objective criteria to the task in hand. The language of literary criticism often confuses description with evaluation and, when pressed to give reasons for our conclusions of approval or disapproval, we are in danger of marshalling apparently impartial evidence which in fact turns out to be judicial. Our conclusions risk being embedded in the evidence, leading at its worst to tautologies which amount to saying that something is effective because it is effective. This is to argue that a war poem is moving simply because war is an emotive subject, or that a sonnet is successful because it contains fourteen lines.

Students themselves sense the inevitability of judgement, with all its problems, in their often irritated defences such as 'it's all subjective anyway', or 'that's just what you [the teacher or lecturer] say'. Yet if your criticism plays safe, and confines itself to purely descriptive observation – saying, for example, that the blank verse in front of you consists of unrhymed lines each of ten syllables – it gets you nowhere in meaningful involvement with the literary experience.

The existence of objective criteria from which sound evaluations can be evolved has been called into question by much modern critical thought. In an article in *The Times Literary Supplement* back in February 1980, Professor John Carey of Oxford University began with the observation that 'the dislodgement of "evaluation" has been effected with remarkably little fuss'. However, this view has not been universally accepted, and we need to trace the path by which judgements are reached.

Consensus of opinion is ultimately what carries the day. This is likely to be affected by all sorts of influences: that of a teacher or lecturer over his or her students, or that of anything you read to help your studies (including the book you're reading now!). An enlightened and sensible attitude is to appreciate that it is out of group discussion, guided by the greater experience of the teacher or lecturer, that reasonable conclusions are gained. For, really, the only road to competence in this scheme of practice, the only road to maturity (a favourite word of the senior figures in practical literary criticism) is through continued exercise. This itself suggests that the workings of literary criticism cannot be reduced to some clinical skills which are easily and quickly acquired. The consensus we speak of is influenced by a whole range of ideological, social, and historical factors which shape the situation in which the appreciation is taking place. But, although we cannot determine the exact nature or boundary of these complexities, this does not mean that we should not be aware of their presence. At the very least, for example, we can sense that Shakespeare will be read differently in different geographic, historical, political and class surroundings. Although all students are, of course, not identical, the ideal of examination work is to elicit an intelligent uniformity of response. Naturally, if this were to happen we would all get the same marks. Ability will always vary, but it is ability which most searchingly applies critical skills which will be most amply rewarded.

This means that external considerations which influence reader response must be recognized but kept in check. These include the pace of our reading, our mood at the time, and the associations words have for us beyond the use made of them in the text. The discipline needed is to try to focus upon the part that language plays within the work in hand. By this means a canon of supposed literary excellence has accumulated through thousands of years of classical and modern literary production. The qualities enshrined in this literature are thought to testify to the existence of norms to which we all – reader, critic and artist – subscribe. So a question on *Macbeth* which asks 'How successfully does Shakespeare dramatize the conflict between good and evil?' takes it for granted that there are absolutes of 'good' and 'evil' which it is likely that Shakespeare has in some measure effectively expressed in his tragedy.

Faith in the existence of abiding standards has been questioned by a number of different critical approaches, some of which we touch on in section (iii). In broad terms this could be seen to be linked to the political condition of the world we live in, where individual liberty, or licence, is valued over and above authoritarian constraints, be they ever so enlightened. Some literary/critical versions of this state of affairs do take the reader's response into account. Each reading of the text is considered to be worth attending to as an integral part of critical engagement. In its more radical manifestations, this leads to the idea that literary categories, and the qualities which are thought to derive from them, are impositions upon material which inhibit the reading process. If, then, we go a step further and take individual reactions as the sole guide to literary judgement, we might find the pulp prose of the daily tabloid preferred to the works of Shakespeare.

(iii) Theories

The essential ingredient for excellence in practical criticism has been generally thought to be complexity. The classic treatise in this case was and remains William Empson's *Seven Types of Ambiguity*, first published in 1930. He dismantles and reassembles texts as if they were watches in order to see what makes them tick. From his example we are meant to learn the skills of literary analysis. But the analogy breaks down because the detailed complexity of literature, with all its social and historical ramifications, will not yield to the circumscribed, mechanical dimensions of a wrist-watch. In the final analysis literary criticism cannot be reduced to scientific practice upon finite material, no matter how much the terms of its discourse might betray a yearning to claim that kind of status. Our experience of students' queries about set texts, particularly Shakespeare, is instructive here. Their questions sometimes presuppose an 'either/or' solution to the problem they face (e.g. 'Is Macbeth foredoomed or does he have free will?'). But life admits of no easy answers, nor does Shakespeare. Indeed, doubtless it is because Shakespeare and other major writers are so complex that a desire for secure guidelines is revealed in this type of question. It is important to realize that honest doubts, reached after a thorough and responsible inquiry, are by no means a confession of inadequacy. On the contrary, the seeing of all sides to all questions is likely to lead to genuine uncertainties, which it would be unfortunate to resolve through crude conclusions.

Here we face the problem of the relationship between literature and life. In the eighteenth century, that great and influential critic Dr Johnson affirmed that Shakespeare held a 'mirror up to nature'. The concept is not as simple as it sounds, for it assumes that the reflection and the object are the same. Still, despite the challenges of much contemporary theory against such a common-sense view, the yardstick of quality which implicitly underpins the kind of literary experience to which most of us own, and which informs the practice you are engaged in, is one that sees the words on the page as reflecting the human condition beyond it – a reading which, in effect, emphasizes 'what' is said over 'how' it is said. This is conspicuously evident in the popular reading of novels, where the stylistic and rhetorical manner of presentation is much less readily apparent than it is in poetry or verse drama. Yet 'how' things are said, the manner, inevitably conditions 'what' is being said, the content, in all writing. The familiar concept of a 'good read', however, would seek to do away with the effort of analysis; for the sentiment that analysis is not only unnecessary, but actually harms the reading process, is commonly held. Historically, this has led to chronic disagreements between critical and creative practitioners. The poet Wordsworth was not alone when he protested that we 'murder to dissect', and we often encounter students who have heartfelt complaints about the ruinous effects of pulling things to pieces. We are sympathetic, yet retain a faith in the enhancing process of literary criticism. As with so many things, added pleasure is only won through effort, and often we all prefer an easy time. It is certainly our hope that you do not see the tasks before you as merely onerous, but as actually deepening the pleasure of reading.

The consequence of the common-sense view is that literature is generally felt to be effective if it appears to be a distinctive reflection, based upon cautious consideration of its stylistic procedures, of the widest range of what is known, or thought, to be the complex of real-life experience. These days some critics call all this in doubt. They see language as possessing an infinite play of resonances where no meaning can be fixed or, as they say, grounded. That literature imitates life is still a widely-held view. But what if, as Oscar Wilde half playfully, half profoundly, supposed a century ago now, it is life which imitates literature – if, say, in dwelling bitterly upon the supposed infidelity of a partner, it is your own reading of love poetry which helps to form your 'real life' reflections, rather than the other way round? For the more experienced in reading you become, the more the dividing lines between literature and life dissolve; and although the study of literature is not intended to turn you into psychotics, with no grasp upon reality whatever, it surely encourages you to see the novel, the poem, drama, essay, in meaningful cross-fertilization with your experience of life.

But what if we go further than Wilde and consider the idea that life itself is a rhetorical construct made up of infinite possibilities of meanings? One thing you would notice in the notoriously difficult language of contemporary theory is the frequent use of words in quotation marks to signal a meaning different from the norm. Here you will see that we have employed the word 'meaning', whereas some modern theorists would maintain that no final meaning is possible – hence the difficulties of understanding them. This kind of theorist is obliged to use language to which the world attaches meaning and stability, while at the same time denying that language can indeed reveal them. The term used for all the complicated manifestations of this type of thinking is itself quite straightforward – deconstruction – and although we have no wish to burden you unnecessarily with new approaches, we are aware that something of these unsettling developments – purposely set against the humane processes of the type of criticism which largely informs what you are learning – has by now influenced the whole area of reading experience, be it ever so obliquely. To have been introduced to these issues, together with the other critical strategies we shall touch on in this section, will certainly help those of you who go on to, or already attend, further education institutions. From the broadest historical and cultural survey of the writings of the Western world, the deconstructive critic sees language deployed on the assumption that it denotes the world beyond. It is this assumption which he or she seeks to challenge. Language then takes on the form (if that is the right word) of a kind of black hole, with no world beyond to reach. Whether that world and its events really exist is a question that is compromised from the start by the very language in which it is asked. So it is that all experience is 'text', or textualized. Conceive of this alongside the idea of an infinite play of meaning, and you begin to see how bewildering it all becomes.

This recent critical development began with a distrust of what was seen as the mere exercise of sensibility on the literary text. Theorists searched for a new cohesion. Impressed by practitioners in another field, anthropology, who had deduced patterns of signs in the study of primitive cultures to which particulars might be referred and by which they might be explained, they looked to the forms of linguistic science as a means of finding and imposing an order upon language. They sought an underlying pattern, or structure, to which all expression could be related and by which it could be clarified. This became known as structuralism, which even made popular news a few years back when literary critics in the humane tradition took up arms against its supporters.

It was not only traditionalists who challenged the structuralist assumptions. The deconstructionists (some of whom were themselves reformed structuralists) objected to awarding the idea of 'structure' itself a specially privileged place outside the shifts and slides of language, when everything should be cast into the melting pot. All language, they declared, is subject to the play of *'différence'* – a French word that cannot be precisely translated into English but which suggests that all words are realized merely by their difference from all others. Consciously using the pun *'différence/différance'*, all attempts to fix meaning, in the relentless succession of past, present and future, are forever deferred – *'différance'* a coinage from the verb *différer* where it means 'to defer'. Thus it is that the term 'misreading' has been coined for the reading of texts, to emphasize the point that all readings are necessarily incomplete and therefore never established. The whole activity of reading has been likened to games play, even erotic pleasure, which does away with the notion that any settled values can be derived from, or imposed upon, the written word. While traditional critics would themselves insist on pleasure in the practice of analysis, you can see that theirs, deriving from the belief that form and content are open to secure scrutiny, is of a radically different nature.

What you will appreciate is that literary practice and the theory it entails do not stand still. Practical criticism, however, which has sustained its momentum for sixty years, continues to flourish alongside shorter-lived approaches. Structuralism has been largely overtaken by post-structuralism, which in its turn – notwithstanding how final it has seemed to be – is losing ground in favour of new historicism, or new pragmatism, which seeks to regain stability by siting the text as a product of race, milieu and moment. These are examined with a view to the needs of a new generation of readers. This movement reflects a growing dissatisfaction with the way in which deconstruction denies any affirmation whatsoever. If all language involves constant deferral of meaning, then all words enter a morass not so much of *différance*, but of indifference. This, it is argued, is simply not true to experience.

Even as deconstruction was gaining influence, other critical ideas were being formulated which locate language firmly within social context. Of these, perhaps feminism has been the most significant. Feminists see language as a male property created by a society which has been traditionally male-dominated. Language has therefore been concerned with male qualities and achievements, either reducing the female world to marginal status or viewing it through a masculine perspective. At its most forceful, feminism sees no reconciliation possible between the sexes, and then a tone of what might be called enlightened hostility informs critical feminist practice. For where the male writer, creative or critical, tries to open his writing to female values he cannot avoid assimilating women to male structures and standards, thus exercising a false chivalry which only serves to extend patriarchal control. So the feminist is forced into her own assertive reading of the text.

But just as one can trace the broad history of literary criticism, so within particular movements it is possible to chart developments. Whereas, in its early days, feminism excused the apparent inferiority of women's writing because men controlled the world and its powers of expression, as it has gained momentum and confidence the female writer has been accorded equal, if not superior, status. This revaluation can certainly be seen in revisions of course curricula and syllabuses. For, against the odds, women writers have vindicated female experience as legitimate territory. Not the least of the benefits has been to provide a radical critique of male-dominated society.

Marxist critics also resist the destabilizing endeavours of the deconstructionist. They seek to establish the ways in which a text is both product and critique of the society which has given rise to it. Within a political framework which sees progress towards a classless society as both inevitable and ideal, the Marxist critic rejects any notion that a text's excellence resides in its universality. To attribute value on those grounds is to confirm a conservative world and the moral systems which support it. Rather, he or she approves of the social and historical placing of texts as essential for demonstrating their relevance to the political movement of their times. In a propagandist sense, Marxist criticism assigns value according to the detection of effective content in the political struggle towards the classless ideal: once it has served its turn, literature can be consigned to the dustbin of history. Critics of Marxist theory argue that there is a contradiction in expecting a work of literature faithfully to represent the society from which it has emerged, and at the same time demanding that it radically take its part in moving the world onwards from the conditions it describes. At its best, however, a Marxist overview can provide a useful corrective to the all-too-familiar assumption that a text piously mirrors the universals of the human condition, which are essentially unmoved by the economic and political environment in which they operate.

This belief in universals is, at base, the liberal humanist position. By claiming that literature deals in universals – expressed in the largely timeless stylistic practices of the writer's art – the liberal humanist feels free from any taint of ideology. Marxists and other radicals counter by arguing that ideology is inescapable. Built into the very evasion of commitment is, subtly, paradoxically, a form of commitment that the Marxist finds particularly unpalatable. This takes the form of an ideological endorsement of timelessness, and therefore conservatism, or the *status quo*. Conflict, dialectic, as the essential element in the political progress of humanity, is thereby discounted.

But even Marx himself allowed that the complexities of literature might lie outside even the broadest political frame-work. Confronted by Marxist criticism, liberal humanist criticism is itself developing its own rejoinder. It argues, for example, that total emphasis upon the political organization of society, giving rise to texts through the medium of authors, reduces the rôle of the writer. Human beings become simply (as some physiologists have argued) mechanical reflections of the world they inhabit and which inhabits them. This limitation of the artist as individual could be seen to be an unwarranted and unproven confinement of the powers of imagination. The conflict here is tantamount to a conflict of political ideology.

A very different method which has gained controversial currency is that of the application to literature of psychological theories. The literary psychologist strives not to take the text at its face value, preferring to see it as betraying meanings beneath the surface indicative of the writer's psyche and the society his or her anxieties represent. Again, this can prove a refreshing way of looking at texts, but it needs to be treated with caution. An uncritical acceptance of any of the approaches we refer to could tempt you away from the traditional critical method into easy speculation, when the discipline of concentration upon the words on the page provides the opportunity for responsible observations which seem capable of being verified. Even when measured against the conclusions of a celebrated analyst like Sigmund Freud, the psychoanalytical approach is open to the objection that its treatment of literature is impertinent. It implies that the writer did not know what he or she was writing, and licenses the all-too-knowing critic to see the text as a kind of elaborate irony at the writer's expense. In its more reasonable guises, however, it extends the possible layers of meaning beyond cautious surface evidence, and attempts to resolve intriguing discrepancies in a writer's work which forever challenge us in any engaged reading of literature.

Yet it is arguable that psychoanalytic criticism can only be conducted when we are familiar with the author's life and works. For example, one critic has related the killing of the albatross in *The Ancient Mariner* to the poet Coleridge's mother, the poem rising out of the subconscious in this particular instance to reveal deep levels of the poet's personality. Exercises in practical criticism, by definition, do not provide students with sufficient information to pursue such ideas.

One leading critic has combined the notion of the entire world as text – as explained in the earlier paragraphs on deconstruction – with psychoanalytic theories to the effect that all literature reveals not the world it appears to describe, but the writer's inmost struggles to come to terms with his or her precursors, the writers and works which have preceded his or her own efforts to say something new. This insight also gives exciting, if complicated, new life to the established method of looking at texts from the point of view of their sources and influences. Similarly, this is unsuitable for the limited field of practical criticism, and can only be profitable in literary criticism for the more experienced reader.

Biography and autobiography, though also of limited relevance to the discipline of practical criticism, do furnish an additional perspective for the interpretation of books. Of the two, biography seems to have the advantage of impartiality, whereas autobiography might reveal more of the personality at close quarters. But you will recall we maintained in the Preface that all writing is literature. From this standpoint it would be best to treat both these forms carefully. The style of presentation might well distort the truth. In our own modest ways we are all aware, perhaps, of the temptation to sacrifice a strict record of events to an entertaining account of them.

Both biography and autobiography, however, can resolve matters of fact. To take a simple example, it would be mistaken to find a writer's experiences in Venice reflected in his or her novel, if letters or journals proved the novel to have been completed, and never retouched, some period before the excursion to Italy. What all psychoanalytic or biographical approaches tend to encourage is an appreciation of the work as a discovery of the person who wrote it. In an examination context which focuses upon passages or set texts you need to concentrate upon the work rather than the author.

All these critical approaches, of course, are not often found in any pure form. The resilient reader will embrace whichever he or she at the time finds appropriate, frequently modulating from one to the other in the writing of any one piece. We shall not confuse you by elaborating on possible hybrids; but simply emphasize that if you can absorb what we have said it will serve as a useful precondition for your own reading, and make your literary work more satisfying both to yourselves and to your examiners. We urge you to think about what you are doing. A firm grasp of first principles instils confidence for most endeavours and literary criticism is no exception.

(iv) Practical advice

Naturally enough, students are always on the lookout for the secrets to examination success. We do not wish to disappoint you, but it has to be admitted that there are no secrets. Indeed, you can take heart from the fact that what we have to say here is by no means entirely novel. It will largely complement what your own teachers and lecturers advise, and afford you the security of knowing that we all – teachers, writers, examiners – think here along the same lines. There is little, if any, chance of your being misinformed. Equally, it will convince you that there is no mystique attached to the practice of good and rewarding literary criticism. The disabling of students by the suggestion that there are mysteries in the craft can be traced to the more pretentious forms of literary élitism which some critics of all persuasions have paraded. In a recent book published by the Clarendon Press called *Beyond*

Deconstruction: the Uses and Abuses of Literary Theory, Howard
Felperin (an American professor now teaching in Australia) has a first
chapter entitled 'Leavisism Revisited', with an introductory section
'The Mystification of Plain Talk'. F. R. Leavis was the most distinguished of the English critics who confidently evolved humane judgements from practical literary criticism – at one point in his career
running a periodical significantly called *Scrutiny*. Felperin satirizes the
sloppier followers of the tradition established by this senior figure. The
extract which follows, describing Felperin's reactions to their writing
and their conversation, would be straightforwardly comic were it not
for the damage that these kinds of pronouncements have caused:

> What I discovered was that an author's prose can be 'crisp', or if he is not
> careful, 'brittle'; his moral outlook 'buoyant' and 'life-affirming' (unless of
> course it is 'life-denying'); his work 'central' or 'essential' or 'marginal'.
> (To what and for whom was not made explicit, unless it was 'life' or the
> 'great tradition'.) The only authors who seemed to be consistently
> regarded as 'central' and 'essential', for whatever it is worth, were
> Shakespeare and Jane Austen. The critic, in turn, supposed himself to
> write out of his 'inward possession' of the work, to seek a 'realized
> experience' in it, to strive for 'completeness of response' to it, but most
> often seemed to entertain 'worries' about its artistic, and especially, its
> moral status until he could finally dismiss it as 'easy' or 'unearned' or
> 'self-indulgent'. He thereby proved himself a reader or critic — never an
> interpreter or scholar or even student — of 'sensibility' and 'judgement',
> superior by implication to the author he had just put in his place.

Professor Felperin's confidence and experience entitle him to be dismissive. But the danger is that if less practised students are awed by the
vocabulary of 'polite' criticism, they will regard themselves, rather
than the criticism, as inadequate. An English professor, John Lucas,
writing recently in *The Times Literary Supplement*, lends his support
to the effort to break down persistent false notions in favour of a
clear-sighted and progressive look at literature:

> There are still a number of belletristic wine-tasters of literature who offer
> for inspection a 'refined' taste, as though it and the 'poetic sensibility'
> that goes with it can be said to exist as something other than an attempt
> to place prejudice beyond the reach of argument. For this dying breed
> the text remains a sacred mystery, to be worshipped from afar, and
> always under the instructions of the high priests of the temple. It is no
> doubt painful for them to realize that their attitude to the text is itself a
> matter for inquiry. But so it is, and indeed the major revolution of the past
> twenty years has been focused precisely here: on attitudes to or relation-
> ships with the text. To speak with what I hope is permissible looseness,

the impact made by feminist criticism and structuralism — often inextric-
able, sometimes breaking apart from each other — has been to demon-
strate that the proper subject for literary studies is not so much text as
the relationship between text and reader, and that the text cannot be
said to have a meaningful existence outside of that relationship.

In order to clear the way for your relationship with the text we now
offer some direct advice.

(a) What you need to do – what we all need to do – is to read
carefully and cautiously. This might well seem an obvious thing to say,
but it cannot be stressed too much. So many errors arise merely from
faulty reading; and nothing could be more irritating than to get things
wrong, not from any understandable miscalculation, but from a mistaken reading of the words and punctuation. And this applies as much
to questions as to extracts. Try to realize all the implications of the
questions posed in any examination, as much as the meaning contained
in any passage facing you. The discipline required here is difficult to
command under examination conditions, but do pay particular attention to the syntax – and punctuation – as a guide to understanding.
Where an unseen passage is concerned, we would recommend three full
readings before committing pen to paper (apart from making notes *en
route* as points strike you).

(b) In any work it is not so much *what* is being said that is of interest,
but *how* it is said. To put it another way, the 'how' always conditions
the 'what': the form shapes the content. Be alert to unusual ways of
putting things, and keep on asking yourselves the difficult yet rewarding question 'Why? . . .'. It will be easier to avoid writing a bald
synopsis if you keep in mind that each choice of word, or stylistic
effect, has been made in preference to a range of other possibilities.
Your job is to decide upon the aptness of the choice. Throughout your
reading aim for what one distinguished contemporary theorist and
critic has called 'that one thing needful for good reading: recognition of
small significant details in a text whether of theory, philosophy, or
fiction, that go against its apparent thematic assertions'.

Do not waste your own precious time (and the marker's) with lame
technical descriptions which fail to say anything about the effectiveness of the work from a critical or aesthetic point of view. If you know
that a Shakespearian sonnet consists of fourteen lines of three quatrains
with a concluding couplet, and a rhyme scheme abab, cdcd, and so on,
do not employ this as a fill-up should you confront one. It is how the
poet exploits the form to express meaning which is your real subject.

(c) Avoid writing down anything you have read or been told which
you fail to understand. Use what technical terms you might possess in
the interests of critical discussion. Do try to get to know some. Used
confidently and creatively they add sophistication and precision,

resulting in an economy of writing which cuts down on ungainly elaborations. Yet be careful not to wield terms of whose meaning you are
unsure, or which you have never really thought about. If you use
words like 'irony' or 'symbol', be sure in your own mind – perhaps
from class discussion – what you mean by them, and make sure this is
clear to your reader. Also avoid emotive terms such as 'atmospheric' or
'poignant'. They are vague, and betray unease and a hollowness of
response. We have helped by providing a glossary of the literary
terms we have used which are not always explained in context. There
are many dictionaires readily available which could supplement our
list.

(d) Hollow responses can be spotted a mile off. By no means believe,
as a rule, that you must inevitably be facing some jewel of English
literature, which demands your lip-service of approval, your forcing a
reaction in glowing terms, perhaps along the lines critically alluded to
in the passage we quoted from Professor Lucas. Of course you might
well feel rightly and sincerely enthusiastic, but even so watch out for
the use of empty superlatives, empty adjectives which say nothing
about the text itself. Ensure that the choice of your terms derives from
your analyses. And do, generally, avoid the use of slang or collo-
quialisms. Where set texts are concerned the chances are that you will
be engaged with works which are highly regarded, but 'even Homer
nods', and you may offer the occasional measured censure if you feel
that it is necessary. Where unseens are involved, it could well be that
you are confronting something less distinguished, and it is for you to
weigh the points of excellence and ineffectiveness. As a general rule,
however, too many students seem to think that they have got to say
something approving, when their hearts are not really in it, and betray
themselves into conspicuously unfelt writing when doing so. This can
be evident in unseens, where there is such a need rapidly to say at least
something; and it is often detected at the ends of essays when, tired,
anxious to come up with a substantial conclusion, the student makes a
final, self-defeating effort to gain more marks. It is all too obvious
when a student is threshing around to get into the material in question,
and equally so when he or she is loath to leave it. Make conclusions
emerge from the substance of your criticism, where your debate has
adopted a logical and interestingly argumentative manner. Over all,
aim for an honest reaction. Merely saying fine things will not in itself
gain extra points – on the contrary. But, by the same token, shock
dismissive tactics will be equally counter-productive.

(e) The intelligence you apply to the literary text is no different from
that required in the pursuit of other disciplines. We have countered the
mystique of English 'letters', but we would do well to remind you that
the literary response is not some emotive pulse divorced from other
experience, which temporarily anaesthetizes the intellect. Proceed

methodically, sifting the evidence, as you are encouraged to do in other subjects.

(f) Do try to vary the language of your responses in terms of pace, tone and vocabulary. Attempt to make your inquiries vital and alive. After all, the creative writers themselves are generally trying to interest you, the reader; and it would be unfortunate if your criticism, in its own way, did not reflect that engagement, for in its turn it needs to involve the person marking it. It is likely that any genuine commitment will result in vigorous writing. The familiar essay or examination question, consisting of a controversial statement followed by 'Discuss', is intended to encourage this very quality.

The vocabulary of critical discrimination is rather limited; and it will be to your advantage if the unseens you are challenged by and the set texts you study have been chosen from different literary genres stretching over a broad range of subject-matter and period. Reading widely is always useful in developing expression and vocabulary, and not the least of its good effects is to provide you with a fuller experience of different kinds of writing within which you can locate the passage or text you are dealing with. Much depends on your ability to say things in different ways, so the more you develop this facility the easier, better, and – where time is of the essence – more effective your performance.

(g) In reading beyond set texts you can improve your general literary aptitude by exploring other works of the same authors. For do remember that examiners, teachers, lecturers are only human. Imagine, then, the beneficial effects if, after scrutizining scores of scripts, the wilting marker is suddenly invigorated by a pertinent parallel made between your set text and some other work you have absorbed. Of course there is the matter of balance here, and you must not get side-tracked. But no writing exists in clinical isolation, and there could equally well be fruitful and pointed comparisons to be made between your set texts, and between passages in literary appreciation papers and other writing which could enhance your performance. In conclusion here, the talents you acquire from each section of your studies are mutually supportive if you deploy them cleverly.

(h) Do not necessarily get perplexed if you feel you cannot sum up or say the last word about any book or extract. As we have said, not only is complexity often deemed to be an essential quality of literature, but some literature – particularly that of modern writers – refuses, like life itself, to give you the full picture. Thus there is a contrast to be made, for example, between the comprehensive narrative of a George Eliot novel and the limited point of view of a James Joyce short story. If a work seems to you to be inconclusive, then you could be on the right track.

(i) Finally here, let us repeat what you must have heard, or will hear, frequently. Time is crucial in examinations. Make sure you exploit it to the full by giving the most complete answers possible, but do leave sufficient time to go over what you have written so as to correct those mistakes you will inevitably make in the hurry of composition. Organize your time so that you answer all the questions asked of you. To complete three out of four, say, no matter how brilliantly, can only gain you a mark out of seventy-five per cent.

Not all that we have said here will apply to all of you all the time. And if some points are echoes of advice from elsewhere, to see it in print might help to confirm its importance. The overriding problem as it affects our writing about literature is that criticism tends to separate form from content when the work or passage reveals each to influence the other in an indissoluble whole. The poet Yeats, echoing in his *Adam's Curse* a belief that goes back to Classical times that 'true art is to hide art', shows why it is, perhaps, that we too often neglect form in favour of content:

> A line will take us hours maybe;
> Yet if it does not seem a moment's thought,
> Our stitching and unstitching has been nought.

What we would say is that you try not to lose sight of the unity of the work of art in your own answers.

The poet Yeats's talking of his trade makes us conscious of the fact that we have skirted the problems of authorial intention. Let us make it clear that when we encourage sincerity of critical response, we refer to the reader's relationship with the text, and not the supposed sincerity of the relationship between author and work. Where the text is concerned, sincerity can only be located in the writing in front of the reader and not in any consideration beyond it. For sincerity, as we usually conceive of it, is not a criterion of literary excellence. The poetic effusions of an adolescent in love might well be sincerely felt but, by any standards, in the triteness of their expression fall far short of good poetry; whereas, conversely, the well-wrought pieces of, say, the Romantic poet Byron embody the very essence of sincerity while having been penned by an unrepentant cynic. Hamlet, when challenged by his mother about his seemingly excessive mourning for his dead father, rounds on her by declaring 'I have that within which passes show'. But 'that within' can only be revealed by that without. Intentions are revealed in texts, or not at all. That time-worn comment 'the author has realized his [or her] intentions' is, even were it open to proof, not of literary consequence. Were the author to have written of those intentions elsewhere we could assess the work in question in the light they shed upon it. But whether or not they are found there, we would still have to face the task of literary critical analysis.

(v) Technical tips

To describe the conventions generally agreed upon for the form and presentation of critical writing – what is understood by the term 'scholarly method' – can be an extensive business. But you will appreciate that, in principle, some regularity in the way we communicate is very advisable. It helps us to write efficiently, economically and clearly, besides making the text of our criticism more agreeable to the reader's eye. This last point is of particular importance when, denied the neat and impressive packaging of typescript, or the benefits of word-processor, our arguments rely on handwriting (hastily penned in examinations) to make their effect. In the ensuing examples we have made use of these common practices when appropriate, and have listed the major ones so that you can follow us clearly, and learn (if you do not know already) how and when to apply them in your own work. For, just as we said earlier that it would be sensible for you to master some technical literary terms, so your writing will benefit from learning to apply some of the rules of presentation which are most frequently encountered in critical writing.

(a) Titles

Underline titles of works referred to. This is very important where, say, a play takes its name from the chief character (such as *Coriolanus*) and you run the risk of ambiguity if you fail to adopt this convention. If you refer to the title of a chapter, poem or essay, which is part of a larger volume, place it in double or single quotation marks.

(b) Prose quotations

All prose quotations of no more than three lines should be incorporated into the body of your script within single or double quotation marks. Where there is a quotation within a quotation, use either single quotation marks within double or double within single. Longer quotations should be separated from your script without quotation marks and indented from the margin.

(c) Poetry quotations

All poetry quotations of no more than two lines should be incorporated into the body of your text within single or double quotation marks. Line divisions should be indicated by the sign '/'. Longer quotations should be separated from your text without quotation marks and indented from the margin, following the pattern of the original.

(d) Omissions and additions

If you are omitting a section from any quotation (poetry or prose) you are using, mark this by the use of three dots. If you are including something within any quotation which is not a part of it, enclose the insertion in square brackets.

(e) Line references

For all line references use the appropriate abbreviation l. or ll., followed by the numbering: e.g. l.7, ll.7–14, ll.7–107, ll.37–57, ll.27–107, ll.137–57. After quotations enclose the line reference in round brackets, e.g. (l.5), (ll.15–20). After quotations from drama specify act, scene, and line, but omit the abbreviation 'l.' or 'll.', e.g. (V.i.22–30), (III.iv.3–11).

(f) Emphasis

With handwriting, where italics are unavailable, you should underline for emphasis – but do so very sparingly.

Throughout your writing aim for consistency of notation and you will be on the right lines.

Part II
Analysis of examples

In our tackling of the examples which follow, we are not claiming to have said all there is to say. However, we realize that we have probably said more than you could manage in the trying conditions of the examination hall. We have also had the leisure to produce more finished answers than could reasonably be expected of you. Yet the point should be made, perhaps, that practical criticism has traditionally sacrificed fine style, if necessary, to the needs of analysis. So, do not worry unduly if your own work in this field fails to achieve the polish you aim for in essays on set texts.

We felt it would be unproductive and artificial for us to write exactly in the manner you would need to adopt in responding to examination questions, but we are confident that our manner and methods will prove helpful. What we have done is to write continuous pieces which embrace as many relevant literary issues as possible. We have not tried to be clever at your expense, but hope that what we have to say is challengingly within your grasp. We have not said the last word. It would be impossible to do so even if one wished to. We should like you to react critically to what we have written in the interests of developing your own literary appreciation.

This extract from a post-war novel describes a woman's visit to a doctor's surgery.

> By the time my turn to see the doctor came, my complaint seemed so trivial in comparison with the ills of age and worry and penury that I had doubts about presenting it at all. Reason told me, however, that I must do so, and I did. The woman in white showed me into the surgery:
> 5 Dr Moffat was a harassed, keen-looking young man, with pale ginger receding hair. I felt sorry for him: he must have had a more unpleasant hour and a quarter than I had had. He told me to sit down and asked me what he could do for me, and I said that I thought I was pregnant, and he said how long had I been married, and I said that I was not married. It was
> 10 quite simple. He shook his head, more in sorrow than in anger, and said did my parents know. I said yes, thinking it would be easier to say yes, and not wishing to embark on explaining about their being in Africa. He said were they sympathetic, and I smiled my bright, meaningless smile and said Fairly. Then we worked out dates and he said it would be due in
> 15 March. Then he said he would try to get me a hospital bed, though I must understand there was a great shortage, and this and that, and had he got my address. I gave it, and he said was I living with my family and I said No, alone. He said did I know about the Unmarried Mothers people in Kentish Town, and I said Yes. They were very nice and very helpful
> 20 about adoption and things, he said. Then he said that he would let me know about the hospital bed, and would I come back in a fortnight. And that was that.

The opening of the paragraph sets it firmly in the familiar world of ordinary experience, that of spending time – an hour and a quarter, we are told at line 7 – in a doctor's waiting-room before being shown into the surgery. In the company of the old, the anxious and the poor, the narrator has come to regard her own 'complaint' as relatively unimportant. The setting is recognizably modern, and the sentiments are likely to have been shared by many people.

It is when, in mid-sentence, we are told that the narrator is unmarried and possibly pregnant that the passage suddenly gains a sharper focus. (Since this is an excerpt from a novel, it may be the case that the reader already knows of the narrator's pregnancy; but, taking this passage in isolation, we can fairly make a point about the element of surprise.) Retrospectively, her use of 'complaint' seems to be a simple irony: flu or a cold may be rightly so called, but can pregnancy? Perhaps she is using the word 'complaint' euphemistically, out of embarrassment. This may, too, explain the breathlessness of the sentence at lines 7–9, where a succession of 'and's gives an air of hurried automatic questions and answers. Are the narrator's feelings being suppressed beneath a series of ostensibly emotionless statements? Her next sentence, 'It was quite simple', may be read as an expression of relief at having done something which she has had to steel herself for. However we interpret the tone here, it is quite clear that her 'complaint' is not 'trivial', since it raises important moral and emotional problems for her.

But these problems are in no way engaged by the rest of the paragraph, in which the initiative is taken by the doctor, who asks questions, calculates the time of birth, talks about arranging a hospital bed, and gives advice about whom to contact for help with adoption procedures. The doctor deals, that is, in facts and practical arrangements; and his language becomes vague when it moves beyond such matters (the 'Unmarried Mothers people' are 'very nice and very helpful about adoption and things'). His attitude, as presented by the narrator, is clear: he is there to deal with practicalities.

This raises a question about her attitude to him. Does the passage present the doctor sympathetically or is there implied criticism of his lack of sympathy? The novelist has not allowed his or her (the narrator is female, of course, but we do not know if the novelist is) narrator to make any direct comment. Indeed, it may be that the absence of comments reflects the automatic nature of the interview, each character going through the motions in a mechanical, uninvolved manner. It is perfectly possible to argue that the doctor's attention to practical details shows him simply doing his job. That the narrator is just one of many patients makes it clear that he has little time for each one individually. Her lie about receiving some sympathy, at least, from her parents may be seen as absolving him from any obligation to provide it himself.

But there are indications that the novelist has carefully structured the passage to imply some criticism of the doctor. The one expression of real sympathy in the text is the woman's for him: a young man, but with signs of premature ageing ('receding hair', l.6), his harassed state evokes the narrator's 'I felt sorry for him'. She has time, even with her own worries, to sympathize with others. On the other hand, she does not put her emotions into speech. We know of her feelings because she is the narrator, whereas of any unstated emotions he might have we, like the narrator, must remain ignorant. But she then goes on to interpret his shaking his head in a way which clearly invites the reader's judgement. We might miss that she is quoting from *Hamlet* ('more in sorrow than in anger', l.10), an indication of her educated status, but that for him her pregnancy should be a cause of sorrow – better though this might be than anger – seems a very limited viewpoint: the further irony about 'complaint' is that the doctor does appear to treat pregnancy as an illness. It is he, indeed, who, by asking whether her parents are sympathetic, makes the assumption that her pregnancy should evoke sympathy (rather than pleasure, say). Further, his mention of 'adoption and things' may be viewed as highly insensitive: he has automatically concluded that she will not want to keep the child, just as he earlier supposed that someone who is pregnant must be married, even if his question there was simply an attempt at polite conversation.

The novelist's decision to make the doctor a man establishes a pattern of male authority figure and female dependent figure. This hierarchy is present, too, in the distinction made between the anonymous 'woman in white', whose job is to show patients into the surgery, and the named male doctor. An interpretation of the passage which emphasized the doctor's shortcomings, his lack of human warmth towards the woman, could profitably relate these to the idea of gender-based structures of dependency. That the 'complaint' is, of course, a uniquely female experience highlights the consequent problems for a social system in which a man's help is sought by a woman.

Whatever our judgements about the novelist's attitude, they have to be located within a response to the woman's first-person narrative. It is she who, in narrative if not in social terms, controls him, in the sense that the reader's perception of him is entirely through her eyes and ears. Speeches throughout the passage are presented in reported, not direct, form, even when the words are written in a way which approximates to direct speech (e.g. 'He said were they sympathetic' combines the form of reported speech – 'He asked whether they were sympathetic' – with the content of direct speech – 'He said, "Are they sympathetic?" '). The effect of this is to remove any real sense of the doctor's own speaking voice, rendering the entire interview in flat, matter-of-fact exchanges.

The tone of the whole paragraph is, given the very real human problem it deals with, emotionless. The syntax largely consists of simple, unelaborated statements linked together by the simplest of all conjunctions, 'and' (which says nothing about the relationship between clauses or sentences other than that one succeeds the other). This makes it difficult to pin down any distinct attitude towards the scene, even on the part of the narrator. Her final 'And that was that' could reflect her own dispassionate attitude or be her own reflection upon the doctor's dispassionate attitude. If the latter is the case, criticism of him might be implied. If the former is the case, we may wonder whether it suggests a conscious or unconscious suppression of real feelings. The detached style hides from us the inner world of the characters, leaving us to question their personal and social attitudes.

(ii)

This poem describes how a peculiar affinity grew between a woman and a dead stranger.

A Woman's Fancy

'Ah, Madam; you've indeed come back here?
    'Twas sad — your husband's so swift death,
And you away! You shouldn't have left him:
    It hastened his last breath.'

5   'Dame, I am not the lady you think me;
    I know not her, nor know her name;
I've come to lodge here — a friendless woman;
    My health my only aim.'

She came; she lodged. Wherever she rambled
10   They held her as no other than
The lady named; and told how her husband
    Had died a forsaken man.

So often did they call her thuswise
    Mistakenly, by that man's name,
15   So much did they declare about him,
    That his past form and fame

Grew on her, till she pitied his sorrow
    As if she truly had been the cause —
Yea, his deserter; and came to wonder
20   What mould of man he was.

'Tell me my history!' would exclaim she;
    '*Our* history,' she said mournfully.
'But *you* know, surely, Ma'am?' they would answer,
    Much in perplexity.

25   Curious, she crept to his grave one evening,
    And a second time in the dusk of the morrow;
Then a third time, with crescent emotion
    Like a bereaved wife's sorrow.

No gravestone rose by the rounded hillock;
30   — 'I marvel why this is?' she said.
— 'He had no kindred, Ma'am, but you near.'
    — She set a stone at his head.

She learnt to dream of him, and told them:
    'In slumber often uprises he,
35   And says: "I am joyed that, after all, Dear,
    You've not deserted me!" '

At length died too this kinless woman,
  As he had died she had grown to crave;
And at her dying she besought them
0   To bury her in his grave.

Such said, she had paused; until she added:
  'Call me by his name on the stone,
As I were, first to last, his dearest,
    Not she who left him lone!'

5 And this they did. And so it became there
    That, by the strength of a tender whim,
The stranger was she who bore his name there,
    Not she who wedded him.

This poem narrates the progress of a curiously pathetic intimacy
between a woman and a dead man, initiated by critically mistaken
assumptions that both were once man and wife. As is general with
narrative verse, it is the broad outlines of the story which give the poem
its emotional charge, and encourage the reader's involvement in two
complementary ways. We feel the need to fill out the story with detail
on the one hand, and are led to meditate on the larger themes it outlines
on the other. The poem is made accessible through the use of traditional verse patterns and direct vocabulary. A strong rhythmic pattern
dominates throughout, with regular rhyming of lines two and four,
while the repetition of irregular line lengths in each stanza culminates
in a dramatic emphasis on the short six-syllable fourth. It is as though
we are reading a ballad, where the forms of poetry – or verse – stamp
themselves on material often drawn from the lives and language of
ordinary people in order to furnish it with broad importance, broad
significance. The inversions required at lines 21 and 34, 'exclaim she'
and 'uprises he', add to this effect – the quaintness of the latter,
together with 'thuswise' (l.13), suggestive of a sense of folk tradition.

Particulars are edited out – 'She came; she lodged' (l.9) – which
might otherwise detract from the central focus of the narrative. What
stories within stories, for example, are to be glimpsed at in the severe
politeness of the exchange between the two women which comprises
the first two stanzas? The 'friendless woman' (l.7) – never named,
although the taking-on of another's name is a main feature of the
poem – appears from nowhere to find a strangely touching friend in
the very man for whose death she is blamed. Not only is she unable to
absolve herself from stories and social prejudices, but she actually
succumbs to them to the extent that they progressively determine her
own sense of identity. And, of course, the more she finds herself
involved in stories about this dead spectre the more, ironically, she
confirms the community's assumptions. The power of narrative not

just to transform reality, but actually to become reality, reaches a climax in stanza six, where she corrects 'my history' to '*Our* history' (ll.21–22). That she does so 'mournfully' at this stage, however, reflects her ambiguous attitude to the loss of any prior sense of self as she begins to take on redefinition as the sorrowful widow. Although the title of the poem indicates her acquiescence in her new rôle, she proves to be in a situation which is both tyrannical and touching. A firm sense of self, which we know to be false (ll.13–14), is insisted upon (' "But *you* know, surely, Ma'am?" ', l.23) by those who have done most to dislodge it. '[Her] health [her] only aim' (l.8) has proved to be an ironic foreshadowing of the moving but psychologically unhealthy sympathy she is developing for someone she can never know.

Like the reader's access to the entire poem, hers to the dead man is through narrative, through story. This proves so compelling that the whole rich pattern of circumstance assumed as a backdrop has been passed over, leaving only this story to tell the tale. But rather than create a chilling sense of inhumanity, of suspension in mid-air, it encourages the woman to seek for an all-too-human, final unity with the corpse in the grave – much as Heathcliff does with Cathy in *Wuthering Heights*. But in that novel both lovers insist they know one another as well as they know themselves when here on earth. In 'A Woman's Fancy', however, there has been no live intimacy, but a total process of self-effacement which culminates in a pathetic attempt to achieve communion, or gain what never was, in the grave. There are several grim ironies which underline the point. 'The stranger was she who bore his name there' (l.47) but she never bore him children in the wedlock she seeks under the turf. 'In slumber often uprises he' (l.34), yet he is never to rise from the grave. 'And she came to wonder/What mould of man he was' (ll.19–20) who is now mould for ever. The disturbing reflection for the reader is that she has indeed become the widow, for what is the difference between her behaviour and that of a real one? This is highlighted by the fact that we are told the real widow, in contrast, 'left him lone' (l.44). But by this time all distinctions between real and not real have lost their meaning. The woman and the dead man are framed by stories from the start. She assumes a bereaved identity and fancies a dead husband to support it. Whatever is or was the truth, the grounding, remains undefined throughout. All has been subsumed into a new reality developed out of the imaginative power of story-telling.

The story is pitiful, bizarre, but not preposterous. For, on reflection, is it not true that all our lives are caught up in story? Our identities are shaped by the exchanges of everyday life; but what does this come down to but what we are told, and what we tell, of each other? Any sense of basis not only recedes, but itself gets caught up in narrative perspectives as soon as we start to look for it. Thus it is that the ironies of the woman's position in the poem do not isolate her from the rest of us. Rather they point up the similarities of our conditions. Shared burial might signify that something we can call 'real contact' was enjoyed on earth, but this poem prompts the despairing reflection that real intimacy can only be realized when we have passed from the framework of words to our silent rest. In this context the linking of names on the headstone is a chilling reminder that the only certain association is going on beneath the soil.

The woman certainly supplants the wife in name, but through a supreme act of self-denial, of denial of whatever she was beforehand. The central focus is the 'strength of [her] tender whim' recalled at l.46. In appreciating the antithesis of 'strength' and 'tender' within the context of the whole, we recognize the paradox of fragile fiction assuming the strength of reality. This, of course, underlines the *raison d'être* of the entire poem. Through the art of the ballad the world is shown to consist of narrative within narrative in which humane assertions, doomed from the start, take on a universally tragic dimension.

(iii)

This passage is taken from a play, where a lord outlines a practical joke which he intends to perform.

> *Lord.* Sirrah, go you to Barthol 'mew my page
> And see him dressed in all suits like a lady.
> That done, conduct him to the drunkard's chamber
> And call him 'madam'; do him obeisance.
> 5 Tell him from me — as he will win my love —
> He bear himself with honorable action
> Such as he hath observed in noble ladies
> Unto their lords, by them accomplished.
> Such duty to the drunkard let him do
> 10 With soft low tongue and lowly courtesy,
> And say, 'What is't your honor will command
> Wherein your lady and your humble wife
> May show her duty and make known her love?'
> And then, with kind embracements, tempting kisses,
> 15 And with declining head into his bosom,
> Bid him shed tears, as being overjoyed
> To see her noble lord restored to health
> Who for this seven years hath esteemed him
> No better than a poor and loathsome beggar.
> 20 And if the boy have not a woman's gift
> To rain a shower of commanded tears,
> An onion will do well for such a shift,
> Which in a napkin being close conveyed
> Shall in despite enforce a watery eye.
> 25 See this dispatched with all the haste thou canst;
> Anon I'll give thee more instructions.
> > *Exit a Servingman.*
> I know the boy will well usurp the grace,
> Voice, gait, and action of a gentlewoman.
> I long to hear him call the drunkard husband,
> 30 And how my men will stay themselves from laughter
> When they do homage to this simple peasant.
> I'll in to counsel them; haply my presence
> May well abate the over-merry spleen
> Which otherwise would grow into extremes.

Here a lord conveys instructions to his page on how to act the part of a lady. Despite his speaking in blank verse (the form we might have noticed elsewhere to be reserved for the nobility in the plays of Shakespeare's period) there is little elaboration of imagery. It would be out of place in giving commands to a servant, the 'sirrah' of l.1 who exits at l.26, especially where they are of such a detailed nature. The desire is to confuse a 'simple peasant' (l.31), repeatedly described as a 'drunkard' (ll.3, 9, 29), into believing that he is a lord himself. The idea is to persuade him that his all-too-real and long-suffered beggary, spoken of at ll.18–19, is only a fevered disease from which he is now mercifully restored. Presumably roused from sleep in his 'chamber' (l.3), he will be particularly vulnerable to the boy page's assuming the bogus rôle of his lady.

Changes of costume and gesture are demanded, 'such as he [the page] hath observed in noble ladies' (l.7). Although his lord's orders are firmly stated, this shift of identity is ironically mirrored in punning, ambiguous language. For example, 'all suits' (l.2) suggests both 'all ways' and specifically the clothes themselves which will help carry the general effect; 'by them accomplished' (l.8) refers to the 'honorable action/ . . . observed in noble ladies (ll.6–7), and the lords' actual accomplishing, or fulfilling, their ladies' destinies, the pronoun working both ways to refer to both sexes and so underlining the mood of the entire passage. The language also hints at the self-consciousness involved in playing the part of a noble lady – fulfilled by their lords for having themselves acquired the grace of 'honorable action' – which casts a further perspective on the artifice the boy page is himself called upon to accomplish. 'Close conveyed' later (l.23) means both 'secretly carried' and 'brought close up', while 'commanded tears' (l.21) relates to the lord's orders and the boy's having 'a woman's gift' to weep at will. The cumulative effect of these ambiguities seems to accuse women – or noble women at least – of unnaturalness.

For if the boy is capable of acting the noble wife to deceive the beggar, as his lord confidently believes (ll.27–34), what might this mean about the behaviour of real ladies to real lords? On the other hand, the designing element anticipated in the boy's performance could be just because he has to act, and, no matter how accomplished, female behaviour will not come naturally. From the language and use of blank verse, we ought to be able to locate the play in the late sixteenth or early seventeenth century, when boys assumed all female rôles in the theatre. With the proficiency we might then assume any boy actor playing this part to have developed in female rôles, the chances are that some critical points at ladies' expense are being made.

Nothing is better designed to suspend the critical inquiry of this simple drunkard, woken in bed, than 'kind embracements, tempting kisses' (l.14). The punning is continued here, with 'kind' meaning both natural – when the advances are anything but that – and kind in the modern sense. But this anticipation of the comedy lacks the impact that its acting-out might achieve. Although the passage tells us much about acting, it is not strictly dramatic (there is only one speaker), which allows us space to relish the ambiguities already explored. It also enables us to observe the darker social and moral implications of the intention when, in the theatre at least, the comic impact of putting it into action might well override any reservations. The anticipated comic scene depends upon all characters, including even the beggar to begin with, being secure in the sense of their own identity, enjoying the discrepancy between what is real and what is false. Yet the context is theatrical, where everything depends upon illusion, the acting out of identities. From this standpoint the divisions between reality and falsehood, security and insecurity, necessary for the comic effect, break down into a confusion where the 'simple peasant' is no more or less a 'simple peasant' than the lord is a lord.

This wider reflection is prompted by the complex confusions alluded to in the passage. Where page-boys act out the character of loving noblewomen to peasants made noblemen, so winning, ironically, the love of their lords (1.5), all sense of identity comes to what is said, gestured – and confirmed by other characters. Unsettlingly, no real grounding – to use a word from our Part I – is to be discovered. When is a peasant not a peasant? When he is a lord. When is a lord not a lord? When, perhaps, he is prepared painfully to deceive a 'poor and loathsome beggar' (1.19), for sooner or later the peasant will regain his 'real' character. This instability of character, then, enlarges into social and moral criticism of an aristocrat played by an actor, whose insensitivity proves he only postures as one. There is an attempt to preserve the comic tone here because the speaker, secure in his own sense of self, fails to realize the implications of what he is proposing, and the disturbing ironies are left to our contemplation.

Similarly, if a servant boy can 'well usurp the grace,/Voice, gait, and action of a gentlewoman' (ll.27–28), then social distinctions look to be very fragile. Nobility is further questioned throughout by the assumption that it resides in external tricks of conduct. And if a peasant can be preferred to the ranks of his superiors by the way in which his supposed household behave towards him, is not this also the way in which the lord's own status is confirmed? What is meant to justify superiority for either sex is grace within, which is disturbingly easily conveyed by mere externals, the pretended female grace of the page. And, in looking for signs of inner distinction where the male speaker is concerned, all we see is ignoble practice upon a beggar solely for the sake of amusement. His intentions, then, ironically undermine the sense of his own status. The dramatist seems satirically to have misapplied the dignity of blank verse, when the vulgar prose we might imagine spoken by his peasant counterpart would be more characteristically appropriate.

When we try to explain comedy the comedy itself is in danger of evaporating, but here it does seem to have serious implications. The lord takes us into his confidence, but by the close we might feel we want to dissociate ourselves. If the rehearsal of his plans does have this effect then we end up sympathizing with a 'simple peasant' who would otherwise seem to be most unattractive. And here a structural similarity emerges, for his being practised upon calls to mind and lays bare the way in which every audience in the theatre is practised upon by actors playing parts. Not only, then, does this reinforce the general relevance of this extract to the conditions of theatre and the social rôles we play in the world beyond; but also, in politely admitting us into his plans as equals, the lord's entire speech has the contrary effect of rudely exposing an equivalence between us and the 'drunkard' whom he wishes to manipulate.

(iv)

The following passages are two different estimations of John Hampden, a parliamentary leader, who was killed during the Civil War in 1643.

A.   Many were the virtues and talents of this eminent personage; and his valour during the war had shone out with a lustre equal to that of the other accomplishments by which he had ever been distinguished. Affability in conversation; temper, art, and eloquence in debate; pene-
5   tration and discernment in counsel; industry, vigilance, and enterprise in action; all these praises are unanimously ascribed to him by historians of the most opposite parties. His virtue, too, and integrity in all the duties of private life, are allowed to have been beyond exception: we must only be cautious, notwithstanding his generous zeal for liberty, not hastily to
10   ascribe to him the praises of a good citizen. Through all the horrors of civil war, he sought the abolition of monarchy, and subversion of the constitution; an end which, had it been attainable by peaceful measures, ought carefully to have been avoided by every lover of his country. But whether, in the pursuit of this violent enterprise, he was actuated by
15   private ambition or by honest prejudices, derived from the former exorbitant powers of royalty, it belongs not to an historian of this age, scarcely even to an intimate friend, positively to determine.

B.   He had indeed left none his like behind him. There still remained, indeed, in his party, many acute intellects, many eloquent tongues, many brave and honest hearts. There still remained a rugged and clownish soldier, half fanatic, half buffoon, whose talents, discerned as yet only by one
5   penetrating eye, were equal to all the highest duties of the soldier and the prince. But in Hampden, and in Hampden alone, were united all the qualities which, at such a crisis, were necessary to save the state, the valour and energy of Cromwell, the discernment and eloquence of Vane, the humanity and moderation of Manchester, the stern integrity of
10   Hale, the ardent public spirit of Sydney. Others might possess the qualities which were necessary to save the popular party in the crisis of danger; he alone had both the power and the inclination to restrain its excesses in the hour of triumph. Others could conquer; he alone could reconcile. A heart as bold as his brought up the cuirassiers who turned
15   the tide of battle on Marston Moor. As skilful an eye as his watched the Scotch army descending from the heights over Dunbar. But it was when to the sullen tyranny of Laud and Charles had succeeded the fierce conflict of sects and factions, ambitious of ascendancy and burning for revenge, it was when the vices and ignorance which the old tyranny had
20   generated threatened the new freedom with destruction, that England missed the sobriety, the self-command, the perfect soundness of

30

judgment, the perfect rectitude of intention, to which the history of revolutions furnishes no parallel, or furnishes a parallel in Washington alone.

We are still, perhaps, inclined to regard the writing of history as an objective pursuit of truth. But any history which attempts more than a bald recital of generally agreed facts inevitably involves the author in decisions about subject-matter, attitude and style of narration. Even the choice of which 'facts' to select (out of a vast range of possibilities) itself imposes a point of view: suppression of details can be as significant as their inclusion. Evaluation thus becomes entangled in a historian's choice of matter and manner.

When, as here, two different writers attempt to sum up a figure of historical importance, we should be on the look-out for disagreements. Yet these two accounts of the character of Hampden appear to be equally praising. Both begin by declaring what seems to be an unambiguous and unmistakable position: passage A by providing an impressive list of Hampden's good qualities, passage B by the device of ascribing to others separately the virtues which are seen to be all conjoined in Hampden. But no two texts are the same: language, syntax, punctuation all create differences by which we can begin to judge the political or philosophical distinctions between them.

The phraseology of the opening sentences of each passage alerts us to potential differences. Passage B begins with a resoundingly epigrammatic assertion, conveyed in plain, direct, almost entirely monosyllabic language. The central word of the sentence is 'none'; and it is Hampden's uniqueness which is the author's main claim. The opening statement is concise and definite, and provides the basis upon which rhetorical embellishments of the same point can be constructed. These elaborations include emphatic repetition ('in Hampden, and in Hampden alone', l.6), the balance of the sentences which, in parallel construction, counter 'Others' by 'he alone' (ll.10–14), and the declamatory rhythms created by these antitheses (as when 'he alone could reconcile' pulls us up forcefully at the moment when Hampden's private harmony of personality turns into a public exhibition of his ability to create harmony in others).

The opening of passage A, by contrast, is insistent, but more circumspect, in its praise. To say that someone had many virtues and talents is to compliment, but not to attribute uniqueness: others may have virtues and talents, too. It also does not preclude the simultaneous possession of vices and incapacities. This does not mean that the text will necessarily go on to ascribe faults to the man; but it leaves it open to do so, whereas passage B forecloses any possibility of defect: to be unique is to be supreme.

The chosen methods of comparison, too, are suggestively different.

Passage B defines Hampden's complete nature by reference to a series of contemporaries. (The context makes it probable that the men listed are from the same historical period, even if our own historical knowledge takes us no farther than identifying Cromwell as another parliamentary leader in the Civil War.) So the partial greatness of others is the yardstick against which the total greatness of Hampden is measured. Passage A illuminates Hampden's valour with radiantly metaphorical language ('shone out with a lustre', l.2), but compares it with his own other qualities, both public and private. The writer's inspection of Hampden is conducted in terms of the man himself, rather than by means of an expansive series of reference points, each with its own impeccable credentials.

Passage B's development is to return to the note sounded in its opening. Hampden's unique stature ('no parallel', l.23) is repeated, qualified only by a final comparison with an equally high and ideal figure from history. Only another century and another country can provide an equivalent: in his age he is unique; for all time he shares perfection with Washington alone. The full circle of the argument admits no dissent: that the conclusion only modifies the opening by adding a supreme comparison, even after a detailed analysis of the subject, emphatically justifies the author's confident assertions. Passage A, however, elaborates its argument by antithesis rather than by repetition. The pattern of individual sentences in the middle of B is the pattern of A in its entirety. But, as we would expect from our observation of the different methods of comparison, the author here makes a contrast between two aspects of the individual man. The colon in line 8 is the mid-point of the passage, separating a first half of praise from a second of reservation.

It is in terms of this reservation, however guardedly introduced ('we must only be cautious . . . not hastily'), that we can look for a political position from which the writer's judgements are being made. The English Civil War, with its confrontation of totally opposed political principles, remains one of those eras of our history which divide historians most sharply. The author of A now makes his or her attitude quite clear: 'abolition of monarchy' and 'subversion of the constitution' (ll.11–12) are parallel phrases set against genuine patriotism. That which some would see as a laudable aim – the substitution of a republic for a monarchy – is a 'violent enterprise' (l.14). The author of B, on the contrary, describes the rule of Charles I as 'sullen tyranny' (l.17) and chooses as Hampden's only match a leader of a later rebellion against the British crown.

It is true that the author of B perceives objects of criticism in the system which replaced monarchy (ll.17–19) – it is, indeed, the absence of Hampden to remedy these faults which he or she laments. The cause of the faults, however, is located in the 'old tyranny' (l.19) (the Stuart monarchy), so that the theory that one extreme creates its opposite by reaction is being implied. The author of A, too, sees this as a possible theory, but defines it in terms of an explanation for Hampden's own faults ('honest prejudices, derived from the former exorbitant powers of royalty', ll.15–16). So the idea cited in B in order to emphasize Hampden's exception from the norm is used in A as a possible cause of Hampden's bad citizenship.

It is, perhaps, debatable whether we read the first writer's refusal to choose between 'honest prejudices' and the less flattering motive of 'private ambition' as a proper confession that there comes a point beyond which a historian's investigation can go no further (as claimed in lines 16–17), or whether we interpret the device as a means of condemning under the cloak of reasonableness. The particular historical example may seem very remote from us, but the wider issues are still controversial, and an exercise which places before us a defence of monarchy and an approval of non-factional republican revolution is likely to provoke differing reactions based on our own honest prejudices. These will probably determine our judgement of the tone of passage A. Evaluation will thus become entangled in our selection of interpretation.

(v)

The speaker in this poem critically narrates an incident which failed to realize its romantic potential.

Inapprehensiveness

We two stood simply friend-like side by side,
Viewing a twilight country far and wide,
Till she at length broke silence. 'How it towers
Yonder, the ruin o'er this vale of ours!
5 The West's faint flare behind it so relieves
Its rugged outline — sight perhaps deceives,
Or I could almost fancy that I see
A branch wave plain — belike some wind-sown tree
Chance-rooted where a missing turret was.
10 What would I give for the perspective glass
At home, to make out if 'tis really so!
Has Ruskin noticed here at Asolo
That certain weed-growths on the ravaged wall
Seem' . . . something that I could not say at all,
15 My thought being rather — as absorbed she sent
Look onward after look from eyes distent
With longing to reach Heaven's gate left ajar —
'Oh, fancies that might be, oh, facts that are!
What of a wilding? By you stands, and may
20 So stand unnoticed till the Judgement Day,
One who, if once aware that your regard
Claimed what his heart holds, — woke, as from its sward
The flower, the dormant passion, so to speak —
Then what a rush of life would startling wreak
25 Revenge on your inapprehensive stare
While, from the ruin and the West's faint flare,
You let your eyes meet mine, touch what you term
Quietude — that's an universe in germ —
The dormant passion needing but a look
30 To burst into immense life!'

'No, the book
Which noticed how the wall-growths wave' said she
'Was not by Ruskin.'

I said 'Vernon Lee?'

This poem dramatically relates a missed romantic opportunity for which the speaker, apparently male, wants to blame his female companion. The impression of dialogue would seem to confirm his evenhandedness in explaining the occasion; but it is important to observe that, really, the speaker is in total control, the sole communicator of the story to the reader. It is not going on in a dramatic present, but happened some time before, and the speaker is editing his rehearsal of it as he chooses. Notice, for example, how at l.14 he decides to let the woman's hurried lines sink from sight (" 'seem' . . . "), only allowing them to resurface at the broken l.30 (" 'No, the book' "). For all appearance to the contrary, then, the poem is a dramatic monologue, employing first-person narration throughout. With first-person narration, be it poetry or prose, it is often the case that it is not *what* is being said that is of interest, so much as *how* what is being said discloses the character of the speaker. This psychological interest certainly looks to be uppermost in a poem dealing with a situation which is fraught with embarrassment, and where the speaker is intent on self-justification. This means that we must also pay acute attention to the poem's involved syntax in order to appreciate its subtleties.

The experience which is supposed to have prompted the poem is irrecoverable. As we said in Part I, there are some critics and theorists who would maintain that all experience comes down to text, or language. Here we can at least declare that, whatever the experience might have been, it would not have been framed by the cleverly unobtrusive couplets in which the poem is written. All life, of course, made into art, involves constraints and control, but here the choice of such an apparently inappropriate poetic form reflects, perhaps, attempts at manipulation on the part of the speaker, despite the impassioned tone suggesting a frankness of approach.

The 'twilight' setting of the first three lines, with later indications of the Italian provenance, Asolo, suggests romantic potential finally and awkwardly interrupted by the speaker's companion. 'Till she at length broke silence' (l.3) says everything and nothing; but the agitated rhythms attributed to her subsequent lines (ll.3–14), her running on from one thing to the next, the uneasy parenthesis, make it clear that she felt some kind of tension. In view of this the 'simply friend-like side by side' must be seen ironically. That is to say, the speaker regards it as an ironic comment upon his own passion. We, however, might well begin to see it as an ironic comment on hers, at his expense. He could be misreading what are evident signs of her interest in him. And is there ever an occasion such as this one which is '*simply* friend-like [our italics]'? Either it begins to look as if the speaker is merely obtuse, with the poet treating him ironically at this relatively simple level; or we detect that the speaker is deliberately trying to disguise his own diffidence, which complicates the subtleties and the ironic texture. For the speaker interrupts with an apparently passionate revelation of his own thoughts, interpreting hers to be spiritual:

                    as absorbed she sent
        Look onward after look from eyes distent
        With longing to reach Heaven's gate left ajar — (ll.15—17)

But could not this equally be an indication of divinely romantic
yearning, to which he fails, or chooses not, to respond? Men are traditionally privileged to make the first move, leaving women most
unjustly compromised if *they* take the initiative. Here, is it that the
woman went as far as she dared in the way we are told she turned her
gaze upon the speaker in ll.26–28, ending in a half-despairing, half-
provoking 'touch what you term/Quietude'? For, despite the poem
giving the illusion of vigorous exchange, the speaker actually said very
little indeed. The first three lines are addressed to the reader. The
woman's words to him thereafter do not, in effect, stop until l.30. For
although his thoughts take over at l.14, the impression is that her
talking continued at the same time, and for an indefinite period, which
he only allows to resurface at ll.30–32. All he 'said', in fact, was the
" 'Vernon Lee' " which closes the poem, in riposte to her rejection of
Ruskin!
     In Part I (and we take this up again in the Question and Answer
section) we suggest that the more you develop your literary experience
the more you will enrich your response; and this, of course, is not
something which terminates at the end of your career in school or
higher education. You cannot be expected to know much, if anything,
about Ruskin, and even less of Vernon Lee; but from what you could
work out about the poem you might realize that the speaker may be
doing one of a number of possible things. He could be playing a male
rôle in supplying a confident answer with evident satisfaction, which is
pitiful if his total lack of response elsewhere has left the woman so
unsatisfied. Or he might be offering a provocative alternative as a
register of the frustration he has paraded over her disregard, which
ironically we might prefer to see as a more complex frustration in the
face of his own felt inadequacy. As it happens, the response is certainly
provocative: Vernon Lee wrote about Italy directly challenging
Ruskin's high-minded view of art and architecture, which the speaker
claims to see reflected in the way the woman looks about her. But his
near silence is pitiful at the same time, and only aggravates the situation in which the poor woman at least struggles to say and do something. The trouble is we are never sure just what is going on. Language
has often been seen as part revealing, part concealing what it wants to
say, and in a poem where so much is at stake the problem is multiplied.
It is also a debatable point whether we can properly speak of irony
where all is relative – where no secure perspective is present against
which we might measure an ironic deflection.
     An exploration of the speaker's imagery further emphasizes the

uncertainty. He first takes issue with the 'wilding' (1.19) from the rush of things the woman has mentioned, which is her 'wind-sown tree/ Chance-rooted where a missing turret was' (ll.8–9). Why choose this? Could it be that the very vigour the 'wilding' possesses aggravates the weakness he is trying to conceal? His own images regress challengingly to the 'flower' of 1.23, a fittingly fragile equivalent for his 'dormant passion', while the gathering momentum through 'rush of life' (1.24) to 'universe in germ' (1.28) is, in the circumstances, pathetic in its dimensions.

At one end 'an universe in germ' – at the other a seemingly passionate man 'unnoticed till the Judgement Day' (1.20). In these few lines he alludes to the beginning and end of time, within which he places this particular encounter. Yet these vistas are not as ridiculous as they might appear. For romantic moments – or the failure to realize them – both in life and art tend to highlight the larger dimensions of life. The tensions in this poem suggest that there are no certainties – all is relative, a question of relationships, conveyed by language and point of view. What would we give for the woman's version of events, for example, but even then would we be any nearer the 'truth'? You might not know much about the 'Judgement Day' allusion – a perfectly natural protestation on the part of the speaker in the context – but, as with the Ruskin/Vernon Lee exchange, you can appreciate the outline. St Paul focuses upon the aspect of its meaning and promise which concerns us when, in *I Corinthians* 13, he says 'For now we see through a glass darkly; but then face to face'. Perhaps there will never be a Judgement Day, but at least readers of novels are given the illusion of getting there beforehand where writers employ omniscient, or allknowing, narrators who play God to expose characters' minds. But here we are dealing with a poem, a dramatic monologue, where – as in life itself – all thought is conveyed by the voice of the speaker. And it is not that dialogue would relieve the dilemma. As with our Hamlet reference in Part I (which we shall have occasion to repeat in the Question and Answer section (i)), in every condition of life that which is within can only be revealed – if at all – by that which is without, not least the language we use. Out of its focus upon convincing psychological details this poem invites the reader to consider universals. No conclusions, as such, are possible. We see 'through a glass darkly' just as much as the two characters in whatever occurred between them. Paradoxically it is the particularly acute attention to form, punctuation, rhythm and imagery that this poem demands which brings the reader to that conclusion.

(vi)

This passage from a short story describes a girl's visit to a bereaved household in the neighbourhood.

Then the door opened. A little woman in black showed in the gloom.

Laura said, 'Are you Mrs Scott?' But to her horror the woman answered, 'Walk in, please, miss,' and she was shut in the passage.

'No,' said Laura, 'I don't want to come in. I only want to leave this
5   basket. Mother sent — '

The little woman in the gloomy passage seemed not to have heard her. 'Step this way, please, miss,' she said in an oily voice, and Laura followed her.

She found herself in a wretched little low kitchen, lighted by a smoky
10   lamp. There was a woman sitting before the fire.

'Em,' said the little creature who had let her in. 'Em! It's a young lady.' She turned to Laura. She said meaningly, 'I'm 'er sister, miss. You'll excuse 'er, won't you?'

'Oh, but of course!' said Laura. 'Please, please don't disturb her. I — I
15   only want to leave — '

But at that moment the woman at the fire turned round. Her face, puffed up, red, with swollen eyes and swollen lips, looked terrible. She seemed as though she couldn't understand why Laura was there. What did it mean? Why was this stranger standing in the kitchen with a basket?
20   What was it all about? And the poor face puckered up again.

'All right, my dear,' said the other. 'I'll thenk the young lady.'

And again she began, 'You'll excuse her, miss, I'm sure,' and her face, swollen too, tried an oily smile.

Laura only wanted to get out, to get away. She was back in the
25   passage. The door opened. She walked straight through into the bedroom where the dead man was lying.

'You'd like a look at 'im, wouldn't you?' said Em's sister, and she brushed past Laura over to the bed. 'Don't be afraid, my lass,' — and now her voice sounded fond and sly, and fondly she drew down the sheet —
30   ' 'e looks a picture. There's nothing to show. Come along, my dear.'

Laura came.

There lay a young man, fast asleep — sleeping so soundly, so deeply, that he was far, far away from them both. Oh, so remote, so peaceful. He was dreaming. Never wake him up again. His head was sunk in the
35   pillow, his eyes were closed; they were blind under the closed eyelids. He was given up to his dream. What did garden parties and baskets and lace frocks matter to him? He was far from all those things. He was wonderful, beautiful. While they were laughing and while the band was playing, this marvel had come to the lane. Happy . . . happy . . . All is
40   well, said that sleeping face. This is just as it should be. I am content.

But all the same you had to cry, and she couldn't go out of the room without saying something to him. Laura gave a loud childish sob.

'Forgive my hat,' she said.

And this time she didn't wait for Em's sister. She found her way out of the door, down the path, past all those dark people. At the corner of the lane she met Laurie.

He stepped out of the shadow. 'Is that you, Laura?'

'Yes.'

'Mother was getting anxious. Was it all right?'

'Yes, quite. Oh, Laurie!' She took his arm, she pressed up against him.

'I say, you're not crying, are you?' asked her brother.

Laura shook her head. She was.

Laurie put his arm round her shoulder. 'Don't cry,' he said in his warm, loving voice. 'Was it awful?'

'No,' sobbed Laura. 'It was simply marvellous. But, Laurie – ' She stopped, she looked at her brother. 'Isn't life,' she stammered, 'isn't life – ' But what life was she couldn't explain. No matter. He quite understood.

'*Isn't* it, darling?' said Laurie.

It is clear from the start that the 'young lady['s]' position is a difficult one. If you come on a sympathy visit carrying a basket, even to a strange household, you cannot expect to be allowed to leave immediately. Laura gives the impression of concern, yet wishes at all costs to remain uninvolved, and this prepares us for her later contradictions when obliged to confront the corpse, which she at once transforms into 'a young man, fast asleep' (l.32). It appears, however, that the mourners feel obliged to invite her to 'walk in', for the description of 'Em', 'Mrs Scott', absorbed in her grief (ll.16–20) indicates how intrusive the visit is. Yet 'Em's sister' does not hesitate. That the narrator speaks of her 'oily voice' (l.7) and 'oily smile' (l.23) seems to reflect Laura's suspicions about the situation she has got herself into. For on one level Em's sister's expression relates pathetically to the deference she feels she ought to pay to a 'young lady' in their 'wretched little low kitchen' (l.9), where she feels the need, even, to apologize for her sister's grief: " 'All right, my dear,' said the other. 'I'll thenk the young lady.' And again she began, 'You'll excuse her, miss, I'm sure,' " (ll.21–22). On another level, however, there could be something insidious in her behaviour. Now Laura has appeared she is going to be made to go through with what her visit should rightly involve – being brought face to face with the corpse. Unfamiliar with the cramped layout of the house, in her desire to 'get away . . . [Laura] walked straight through into the bedroom where the dead man was lying' (ll.24–26). Em's sister gives her no option, and Laura finds her voice 'fond and sly' (l.29). It is interesting to note that her " 'Don't be afraid, my lass' " (l.28) is in marked contrast to her earlier courtesies. Laura's silent capitulation is starkly conveyed in the narrator's isolated line, 'Laura came' (l.31).

Em's sister's reassurance that " ' 'e looks a picture. There's nothing to show' " (l.30) ironically anticipates the way in which Laura meditates on what she finds in front of her. If Em's sister had intended to give Laura a shock she singularly fails, for, anxious to escape from the beginning she escapes now by creating her own picture of the scene. It seems that her defences, her self-indulgences are so firmly established as to preclude any real grasp of the death and its implications for the family for which she is ostensibly concerned. 'Happy . . . happy . . . All is well, said that sleeping face. This is just as it should be. I am content.' (ll.39–40). The fact that this could refer either to his content-ment or to her own suggests how far she has projected her own person-ality on to the dead man. Either might be 'content' at this stage, but what of those left behind, and affected more nearly than Laura? Her 'he was wonderful, beautiful' (ll.37–38) not only shows her, perhaps, seduced by the superficialities of the undertaker's cosmetic arts, but also reflects the superficiality of her visit in the first place.

But apparently it was her mother who insisted on the visit (ll.4–5), and it would be wrong to be too hard on Laura. For what reaction is ever adequate in the face of death? When she muses 'What did garden parties and baskets and lace frocks matter to him?' (ll.36–37) we are reminded once more of the lack of common ground between social classes, and the predicaments of different households. And yet, for all its inappropriateness, it is an attempt on Laura's part to face the futility of life and the immensity of death. 'Laura gave a loud childish sob' (l.42) as she left, but it is a debatable point whether the 'childish' expression of distress reflects Laura's evasion of a chance to grow up. Similarly, her apology to the corpse (l.43) is ridiculous, gauche, but it does suggest, if only faintly, that she has some sense of the impropriety of all things in the face of finality. But with the kind of consolation to be offered by the brother waiting in the shadows there is unlikely to be any further development.

Having come to terms with the scene to her own satisfaction Laura side-steps any more disturbances. With real impoliteness 'this time she didn't wait for Em's sister' (l.44), and proceeds to the encounter with her brother outside. His emergence from the shadows seems to prefigure the imprecision and inadequacy of their subsequent dialogue. For just as we were led to wonder what reaction was sufficient in the face of death itself, so their easy exchange – " 'Was it all right?' 'Yes, quite' " (ll.49–50) – says everything and nothing. What it does invite is two contradictory ways of looking at the brother. Is he sensitively avoiding the aggravation of his sister's feelings, or is he just indifferent to the whole issue? Laura's reactions suggest that something of her experiences has made a deep impression. She might feel the need to lie about her tears to her brother to save him distress, or because from her background that is the kind of thing you need to do with brothers. But her tears do contrast with the 'loud childish sob' of l.42, and hint at the achievement of a genuine sympathy with the grieving woman 'with swollen eyes and swollen lips' (l.17). Disturbingly, however, the writer cleverly suggests the difficulties involved in trying to identify sensitive concern within polite language, which could be seen as just the opposite. There is also the added complication of the male protector having the effect of suppressing meaningful dialogue. For what reasons, then, do Laura and her brother seem to fail to engage? That this is the case is suggested by the way Laura lapses into the 'simply marvellous' (l.55) response she felt as she stood by the side of the corpse.

Once more, however, we are led to ask just what reaction would be sufficient. The passage contains a situation for which all expression, all language, looks banal. This is not so much a question of the world being solely determined by the language which describes it, as discussed in Part I. Rather the passage characterizes a problem frequently encountered in literature where the incident, the event, is thought to be only too real, only too momentous, so that it is language which fails to have the power to encompass it. This dilemma is encountered in the formula 'words cannot express . . .' which is often found in the context of romantic love! Of course, this is sometimes a rhetorical trick (the technical name is 'paralipsis') to add weight to subsequent description; but it can, as treated in this passage, reveal a disconcerting problem. A corollary to this is that if you do find words to express the supposedly inexpressible then you run the risk of limiting its potency.

As if sensing the unsatisfactory nature of her exchange with her brother, and what it has led her to say, Laura tries finally to place her experiences in meaningful perspective. Yet, fixing her tearful eyes on her brother she can only hesitate a half-sentence of the largest possible significance: " 'Isn't life,' she stammered, 'isn't life – ' " (ll.56–57). As question or statement the sentence is incapable of conclusion because we are all incapable of finding adequate language for life and death. What her words do reflect once more is the ambiguous light in which she is cast: is she self-indulgent, or sincerely groping for conceptions which will make sense of her experiences? We are equally unclear about her brother's reply. Does his emphatic echo of her hesitation indicate complacency, unconcern, the delusions of the polite class in its thinking it knows without wishing or needing to inquire too deeply, or does it reflect a genuine sympathy with his sister's disturbances? Ambiguity continuously and appropriately mirrors the uncertainties caused by the realities of life, death, and difficult and delicate social relationships which are throughout the subject-matter of the passage.

(vii)

The following descriptions of alpine landscapes are taken from a novel (A) and a journal (B).

A.   I performed the first part of my journey on horseback. I afterwards hired a mule, as the more sure-footed and least liable to receive injury on these rugged roads. The weather was fine; it was about the middle of the month of August, nearly two months after the death of Justine; that

5   miserable epoch from which I dated all my woe. The weight upon my spirit was sensibly lightened as I plunged yet deeper in the ravine of Arve. The immense mountains and precipices that overhung me on every side, the sound of the river raging among the rocks, and the dashing of the waterfalls around, spoke of a power mighty as Omnipotence — and I

10   ceased to fear or to bend before any being less almighty than that which had created and ruled the elements, here displayed in their most terrific guise. Still, as I ascended higher, the valley assumed a more magnificent and astonishing character. Ruined castles hanging on the precipices of piny mountains, the impetuous Arve, and cottages every here and there

15   peeping forth from among the trees formed a scene of singular beauty. But it was augmented and rendered sublime by the mighty Alps, whose white and shining pyramids and domes towered above all, as belonging to another earth, the habitations of another race of beings.

B.   Before ascending the mountain, went to the torrent (7 in the morning) again; the Sun upon it forming a *rainbow* of the lower part of all colours, but principally purple and gold; the bow moving as you move; I never saw anything like this; it is only in the Sunshine. Ascended the Wengen

5   Mountain; at noon reached a valley on the summit; left the horses, took off my coat, and went to the summit, 7000 feet (English feet) above the level of the sea, and about 5000 above the valley we left in the morning. On one side, our view comprised the *Yung frau*, with all her glaciers; then the *Dent d'argent* shining like truth; then the *little Giant* (the Kleiner

10   Eigher); and the great Giant (the Grosser Eigher), and last, not least, the Wetterhorn. The height of Jungfrau is 13000 feet above the sea, 11000 above the valley; she is the highest of this range. Heard the avalanches falling every five minutes nearly — as if God was pelting the Devil down from Heaven with snow balls. From where we stood, on

15   the Wengen Alp, we had all these in view on one side; on the other, the clouds rose from the opposite valley, curling up perpendicular precipices like the foam of the Ocean of Hell, during a Spring tide — it was white, and sulphury, and immeasurably deep in appearance. The side we ascended was (of course) not of so precipitous a nature; but on

20   arriving at the summit, we looked down the other side upon a boiling sea of cloud, dashing against the crags on which we stood (these crags on

one side quite perpendicular). Stayed a quarter of an hour; began to descend; quite clear from cloud on that side of the mountain. In passing the masses of snow, I made a snowball and pelted H. with it.

The first passage begins in a factual manner, providing information about the conditions of the narrator's journey (means of transport, weather, date). This might lead the reader to think, at first, that the novel is much like a journal. But elements of a more formally literary style are present: the journey is 'performed', not simply 'made', the mule is 'sure-footed', the 'rugged roads' form a satisfyingly alliterative phrase, and clauses and sentences are properly grammatical. A level of language is thus established for the entry, in mid-sentence, of the subjective world of the narrator which is described in elevated terms: 'miserable epoch' (l.5) is more formal – and to modern ears more artificial – than 'unhappy time', and 'woe' is more literary than 'unhappiness' (the *Oxford English Dictionary* describes it as 'poetic or rhetorical').

It soon becomes clear that those opening facts are introductory, serving to set the scene in place and time. They are not information for its own sake, such as a traveller might record in a journal; but provide a context for expression of strong personal feelings. The journey provides the narrator with emotional relief. As he or she plunges deeper into the ravine, so the 'weight upon my spirit was sensibly [i.e. 'in a manner perceptible to the senses'] lightened' (ll.5–6). The sheer power and size of the landscape are matched by an equivalent grandeur of language: mountains and precipices are 'immense' (l.7), not just 'big'; and river and waterfalls are 'raging' and 'dashing' (l.8), the present participles conveying a sense of continuing movement. The descriptive language attempts in this way to replace the 'weight' of the traveller's grief, the intensity of the physical experience of nature taking over from intense emotional experience. Awe at the almighty creator of such immensity is stronger than any merely human emotion: fear of humanity gives way to fear ('terrific', in its literal meaning of 'terrifying') of the works of an all-powerful force ('Omnipotence', l.9).

To enter the Alpine landscape is to enter a world which is literally and metaphorically above the human world. As the narrator ascends higher (l.12) – climbing now to complement the earlier plunge into the ravine – so the world of the valley beneath (ruined castles desperately hanging on to precipices, cottages fearfully 'peeping forth from among the trees', l.15) is left behind. This physical ascent is mirrored within the narrator: grander feelings replace lesser emotions. The peaks of the Alps represent the highest points of the landscape, and they are so far above that they seem to belong to 'another earth' and 'another race of beings' (l.18). The physical ascent ultimately separates the traveller from a merely human world, its emotions being set in their subordinate place by sight of the force which 'towered above all' (l.17).

The second passage also begins with facts: time, colours, and simple scientific observation of the effects of sunlight on water. But there are key differences to be noted. The language is less elevated, more direct, than in passage A, the narrator speaking, for example, not of performing a journey, but of simply going ('went', l.1). Sentences are left uncompleted – the personal pronoun, 'I', is omitted in the opening line – so that the passage is partly in note-form, as in a diary or journal written casually on the spot or soon after the event. Personal details about the writer relate directly to his or her experience of the scene, rather than to an internal emotional world: 'I never saw anything like this' (ll.3–4) is a way of making the rainbow an exceptional event.

The method of writing established at the beginning continues throughout the extract, rather than entirely giving way to more powerful description. So references to time recur at lines 5, 7, 13, 22; and colour is specified in line 18. The writer's interest in scientific accuracy continues as the heights of the Wengen mountain and the Jungfrau are precisely recorded. The direct style, too, is sustained: the narrator 'left the horses', 'went to the summit' (l.6), 'made a snowball' (1.24), in each case choosing the very simplest verb for the action. The note-form is retained, the personal pronoun, for example, being omitted from the series of verbs in the second sentence ('Ascended', 'reached', etc.) and in the penultimate sentence ('Stayed', 'began'). Details about the writer, far from emphasizing personal sorrow and a desire to escape from it as in A, become almost inconsequential: 'took off my coat' (ll.5–6) just tells us that it was a tiring climb, and the final detail of the making of a snowball appears to be just a whim of the moment.

There are, then, clear contrasts of style and attitude between the passages; but to state them in this way is to over-emphasize differences. The imaginative release of A depends in part upon precise description, as the 'white and shining pyramids and domes' (l.17) provide a visually exact point of reference for the final aspiration. Conversely, the scientific accuracy sought after in B is also a means of expressing greatness of scale: an increase in numbers (the Wengen 7000, the Jungfrau 13000 feet above sea-level) is also an increase in grandeur. Further, the narrator of B mingles his or her note-form language with more fanciful descriptions. The Dent d'Argent ('silver tooth') shines out with a simile – 'like truth' (l.9) – which stands out isolated in the passage, too, as its connection of landscape with abstract idea is not followed up. More sustained is the cloud/sea simile (ll.15–21) which, in its comparison of one element in nature to another, is appropriate for those parts of B that echo A's emphasis on the immensity of the scene: 'precipices' (ll.7, 13 in A, ll.16–17 in B; also 'precipitous', l.19 in B), 'immeasurably deep' (l.18 in B, cf. 'deeper', l.6 in A) – a phrase which is all the more telling after the precise measurements given earlier – and 'dashing' (l.8 in A, l.21 in B).

Such similarities, however, give way in their turn to a crucial difference of style and hence of tone. It looks as if B's fanciful image for the fall of avalanches ('as if God was pelting the Devil down from Heaven with snowballs', ll.13–14) is the equivalent of A's 'power mighty as Omnipotence' (l.9). But, rather than elevating the impressiveness of the scene, the analogy with snowballs actually diminishes the divine to a human scale. The tone is more irreverential than awed. Especially is this the case when we recall that apparently irrelevant closing sentence about pelting a companion ('H.' is clearly shorthand for a name) with a snowball. The journal brings the episode down to a human, ordinary level at the end; whereas the novel pursues a consistent process of elevation. Thus, where the narrator in A acknowledges only the mighty power of nature, the author of B generally keeps the experience to a human scale. The measurements of mountains in B, for example, contrast with the impressive but vaguer adjectives of A ('magnificent and astonishing', ll.12–13; 'sublime', l.16). The journal contains its share of powerful adjectives (e.g. 'boiling', l.20); but it literally and metaphorically descends (l.23) from its most energetic description to a mischievously human ending.

Any description necessarily involves the describer in adopting an attitude, a stance towards the object described. This is rendered through the language, tone and structure of the writing. These two extracts share a similar topography, but use it in order to define very different relationships between the 'I' and the landscape.

(viii)

These two poems use different worlds of singing to develop their ideas.

A. *The Street-Singer*

> She sings a pious ballad wearily;
> Her shivering body creeps on painful feet
> Along the muddy runlets of the street;
> The damp is in her throat: she coughs to free
> 5 The cracked and husky notes that tear her chest;
> From side to side she looks with eyes that grope
> Feverishly hungering in a hopeless hope,
> For pence that will not come; and pence mean rest,
> The rest that pain may steal at night from sleep,
> 10 The rest that hunger gives when satisfied;
> Her fingers twitch to handle them; she sings
> Shriller; her eyes, too hot with tears to weep,
> Fasten upon a window, where, inside,
> A sweet voice mocks her with its carollings.

B. *After the Opera*

> Down the stone stairs
> Girls with their large eyes wide with tragedy
> Lift looks of shocked and momentous emotion up at me.
> And I smile.
>
> 5 Ladies
> Stepping like birds with their bright and pointed feet
> Peer anxiously forth, as if for a boat to carry them out of the wreckage;
> And among the wreck of the theatre crowd
> I stand and smile,
> 10 They take tragedy so becomingly;
> Which pleases me.
>
> But when I meet the weary eyes
> The reddened, aching eyes of the barman with thin arms
> I am glad to go back to where I came from.

Poem A describes the life of a destitute street-singer, contrasted with a concluding glimpse through a window at the comforts from which she is shut out. Poem B works the other way round. It focuses upon the 'girls' and 'ladies' emerging from the opera-house, contrasting them in the last three-line stanza with the exhausted barman who has been waiting on them within. The animated tone of poem A is conveyed by insistent iambic rhythms throughout, only interrupted twice – at the beginning of 1.7 and 1.12, dramatizing the words 'Feverishly' and 'Shriller' with strong accents on the first syllable. The close rhyme pattern 'wearily/feet/street/free' changes abruptly after the first quatrain, beginning with 'chest' at the end of 1.5, as if to stress the painful liberation of her voice. This is further emphasized by the harsh sounds 'cracked', 'husky', and 'tear' (1.5), which it takes much effort for us to articulate. We might reflect that real liberty is doomed from the start when the only freedom achieved is the release of the voice that confirms a state of beggary. But, unlike those of poem B, the stylistic effects concentrate on the sufferer's plight rather than on those responsible for it. The poem is a sonnet which divides into two quatrains followed by a sestet; but, in reserving its overt critical point for the last one and a half, possibly two and a half lines beginning 'her eyes . . .' (1.12), curiously the sonnet leans more towards the Shakespearian type, which follows three quatrains with a pointed couplet.

The situation in poem B is less extreme, the tone less earnest, allowing for critical ironies to be developed throughout. Poem A's intensity betrays itself into the stylized, exaggerated 'eyes, too hot for tears to weep' of 1.12, whereas *After the Opera* is more critically incisive through being more subtly stated. The hints are given in the repetitions 'And I smile' and 'Which pleases me' at the end of the first two stanzas, together with 'I stand and smile' (1.9). Against these the 'ladies' are picked out in a line all to themselves at the beginning of the second stanza, with their fastidious behaviour nicely conveyed in the way that the rhythms of the next two lines accent the principal words amid the scurry of connecting language:

> Stépping like bírds with their bríght and póinted féet
> Péer ańxiously fórth, as if for a bóat to cárry them out of the
> wréckage.

For poem B, unlike the insistent metrical patterning of poem A, exploits a mix of free verse rhythms and rhyme to convey its satire. For the sensitivity of the 'Girls with their large eyes' (1.2) not only is undermined by the way in which the barman is singled out by 'weary eyes/ . . . reddened, aching eyes' in the last stanza; but also by the deflating rhyme of 'tragedy' with 'up at me' (ll.2–3). A similar effect occurs in the combination of 'tragedy' and 'becomingly' at 1.10. The satiric, ironical dimensions of poem A are confined to the street-singer's singing a 'pious ballad' (1.1) with the varied description of her abject condition proving piety, charity, to be noticeably lacking. 'Pence . . . will not come' (1.8) and she is left on the wrong side of the glass at the close; where 'carollings' might be intended to mean more than just singing, to expose hypocrisies at Christmastide, supposedly the season of good will.

But just as in poem A the street-singer's pitiful efforts evoke no virtuous response, so the poet's treatment of exclusively the female part of the opera audience in poem B implies that no genuinely sensitive effects have been caused by the experience of high lyric art. The 'girls' and 'ladies' are made to seem oblivious of the kinds of inequalities and injustices that their life-style causes, just as an implicit criticism of the kind of society that lets poor women roam the streets achieves brief definition in the indifference on the comfortable side of the window in poem A. Why does the speaker in poem B spotlight the 'stone' of the 'stairs' at the beginning of the poem unless to go on to suggest that the women are stony-hearted themselves, with a hint at self-conscious or exaggerated response to 'tragedy' according to the differences implied about their age? Girls with 'large eyes wide' are contrasted with ladies who 'take tragedy so becomingly', the latter more intent on their immediate convenience than the effects of opera as they 'peer anxiously forth, as if for a boat to carry them out of the wreckage' (l.7).

The speaker in poem B confuses the art form itself, the opera, with the reactions (or rather lack of them) of its audience; and although the poem excludes male patrons there is no indication that their responses would be any different. This stems from what we call affective criticism – judging the work not in its own terms but by the responses it gives rise to – and is something we allude to in Part I. The temptation to do this is provoked by the poem's settling on an art that is traditionally thought of as élitist. It also treats only of female patrons, when it is women – perhaps with the insidious kind of chauvinism which we touch on in Part I – who are generally credited with a sympathy which men lack. In poem A the plight of the street-singer is at least implicitly a criticism of a society that could do much to relieve her situation and those like her, but just what response is being demanded by poem B's juxtaposing of its females with the tired barman? Not that poem B is unfair, or naive. Rather its sharply realized contrasts are meant to indicate the broad injustices of a social order which brutalizes, with the irony that this is so tellingly depicted in the one place, the opera-house, that appears to be, or should be, most civilized.

We say 'should be' because poem B in particular takes into account the vexed question of how far, if at all, the arts are a force for good in the world. It is this assumption which underlies the literary criticism practised by the liberal humanists whom we mention in Part I, and which is still thought to sanction literary studies in school, college and tertiary education. Here, if musical art fails it is literary art which instructively highlights the deficiency. Both poems work through particular apprehension of things – the telling image – rather than general social philosophizing. This is strengthened in both poems by having the details registered by observers, who in noticing these particular symptoms allude to the underlying diseases. The poems are criticisms rather than solutions. The third-person point of view in poem A gives us an impassioned vignette which at least evokes a general sympathy on the part of the reader. The more dispassionate stance of the first-person observer in poem B conceals a comparable disapproval, which surfaces in the spectacle of the barman in the last stanza and the speaker's leaving the whole scene behind for his own preferred, yet unspecified – and presumably less superficial – point of origin. But in a poem which is so critical of others' self-centredness, the speaker feels no need to befriend the barman. The speaker's refuge in poem A is merely implied from the vantage point of observation. Both impress upon the reader the part they play in the essentially liberal, essentially humane practice of literary art. The terms of both the writing and the reading of these socially conscious poems do not allow for any detailed social reform. They alert the reader to injustice, which is perhaps all that can ever be expected of any kind of art.

(ix)

The following passage is part of an introduction to an essay about human knowledge.

> Our business here is not to know all things, but those which concern our
> conduct. If we can find out those measures, whereby a rational crea-
> ture, put in that state which man is in this world, may and ought to govern
> his opinions, and actions depending thereon, we need not to be trou-
> 5 bled that some other things escape our knowledge.
>
> This was that which gave the first rise to this *Essay* concerning the
> understanding. For I thought that the first step towards satisfying several
> inquiries the mind of man was very apt to run into was to take a survey of
> our own understandings, examine our own powers, and see to what
> 10 things they were adapted. Till that was done, I suspected we began at
> the wrong end, and in vain sought for satisfaction in a quiet and sure
> possession of truths that most concerned us, whilst we let loose our
> thoughts into the vast ocean of Being, as if all that boundless extent
> were the natural and undoubted possession of our understandings,
> 15 wherein there was nothing exempt from its decisions, or that escaped its
> comprehension. Thus, men extending their inquiries beyond their capa-
> cities, and letting their thoughts wander into those depths where they
> can find no sure footing, it is no wonder that they raise questions and
> multiply disputes, which, never coming to any clear resolution, are
> 20 proper only to continue and increase their doubts, and to confirm them
> at last in perfect scepticism. Whereas, were the capacities of our under-
> standings well considered, the extent of our knowledge once dis-
> covered, and the horizon found which sets the bounds between the
> enlightened and dark parts of things, between what is and what is not
> 25 comprehensible by us, men would perhaps with less scruple acquiesce
> in the avowed ignorance of the one, and employ their thoughts and dis-
> course with more advantage and satisfaction in the other.

We expect that an introduction to an essay will set out the author's aims and methods, preparing the ground for what is to follow. This extract clearly does this by defining both the intention of the essay (to discover 'those measures, whereby a rational creature . . . may and ought to govern his opinions, and actions depending thereon', ll.2–4) and the rationale for that intention. The writer is concerned with what it is possible for people to know; and this entails establishing the scope of human understanding. The opening sentence judiciously sets complete knowledge against whatever is relevant to how we lead our lives, dismissing the former aspiration in favour of the latter limitation. 'Conduct' (l.2), as is evident from the rest of the passage, means more than just 'behaviour' in our restricted modern sense. This discrimination

50

between the unachievable and the possible is repeated in the second sentence, but with the order inverted ('If we can find out . . . we need not to be troubled'). The first paragraph is thus a complete, structurally self-contained statement of aims: 'our business is not x, but y. If we can discover the principles of y, we need not bother about x'.

What, then, does the writer want us to think? The basis of the argument is the here and now, human thoughts and actions in the real world ('that state which man is in this world', l.3). This is assumed to be the province of the 'rational creature' (ll.2–3) who should not be concerned with whatever might lie beyond his or her comprehension. So to limit the possibilities of knowledge is actually to take a necessary and positive step forward. Rather than an admission of defeat, it is a sensible playing to our strengths. The writer's carefully structured prose reflects the reasonableness of the attitude. Indeed, it is the means by which the author persuades us of the irrefutable logic of the principles. Thoughtful writing, we are led to think, must express similarly well-considered views. The writer's use of the first-person plural ('Our', 'we', ll.1–2) brings us, as readers, into a shared position: we partake of the logical, sensible argument.

The second paragraph elaborates these principles and extends the stylistic means by which they are persuasively presented. The writer comes across as a judicious reasoner, who is duly tentative rather than dogmatic in manner ('I thought', 'I suspected', (ll.7, 10). He or she is not over-ambitious, preferring to take things in proper order ('the first step', l.7), while intending to be thorough in method ('take a survey of our own understandings', ll.8–9). The need to establish human limitations and work from these is justified by being set against the alternative, which is to take on a task for which we are self-evidently unfitted ('whilst we let loose our thoughts . . . escaped its comprehension', ll.12–16), and which is, in any case, incapable of being completed ('never coming to any clear resolution', l.19). Positive results can only be attained by knowing ourselves, and carefully considering our capacities (ll.21–2).

That these fundamental principles are the sensible ones is, again, suggested by the style. The writer chooses to begin sentences with words indicating logical processes: 'Till that was done' (l.10), 'Thus' (l.16), Whereas' (l.21). Language of scientific observation presents the essay as founded upon a sound basis: 'survey' (l.8), 'examine' (l.9), 'well considered' (l.22). On the other side of the logical divide established in the first paragraph, images are used which forcefully create the impossibility of the alternative procedure. So the careful placing of the need for observing the appropriate 'first step' (l.7) contrasts with the idea of a 'vast ocean of Being', a 'boundless extent' in whose 'depths' we can 'find no sure footing' (ll.13–18). One method provides us with a limited, but certain, foothold; while the other sends us into unfathomable depths. We either hold onto comprehensible reality or drown in the unknown. For a sensible person, such as the writer and the implied reader, the decision is obvious and necessary. The light/ dark metaphor in the final sentence completes the passage's presentation of stark and clearly defined alternatives: we must humbly accept human ignorance in some areas so that our energies are directed to objects of productive inquiry.

It is not the writer's rôle in the excerpt to define what exactly this possible knowledge is. The main body of the essay, we assume, will proceed to explore this. The introduction justifies the author's method as being the only one which is (to translate the metaphor of 'first step' and 'sure footing' into the language of deconstruction) 'grounded' in reality. There are taken to be 'truths' (1.12) which we can quietly and surely possess if we carefully estimate our capacities. Ideas can be neatly divided, as light and dark, into those which may be objectively arrived at and those which may not.

It is the style and form of the passage which seek to persuade the reader of the validity of these assumptions. The logical language, the clearly defined metaphors, the balanced and antithetical syntax, and the inclusion of the reader in the reasoning process are the means by which the 'truth' of the principles is established. If this is achieved, then the reader is persuaded that there is 'sure footing' to be found in the essay which follows. The introduction's success can be measured by the extent to which it allows for no dissent and thus prepares a reader to discuss the essay within the terms which it proposes.

(x)

In this excerpt from the beginning of a play, one character (Aston) has invited another (Davies) into his living quarters. (S.D. = stage direction.)

ASTON.   Sit down.

DAVIES.   Thanks. (*Looking about.*) Uuh. . . .

ASTON.   Just a minute.

> ASTON *looks around for a chair, sees one lying on its side by the rolled carpet at the fireplace, and starts to get it out.*

DAVIES.   Sit down? Huh . . . I haven't had a good sit down . . . I haven't
5   had a proper sit down . . . well, I couldn't tell you. . . .

ASTON (*placing the chair*). Here you are.

DAVIES.   Ten minutes off for a tea-break in the middle of the night in
that place and I couldn't find a seat, not one. All them Greeks had it,
Poles, Greeks, Blacks, the lot of them, all them aliens had it. And they
10   had me working there . . . they had me working. . . .

> ASTON *sits on the bed, takes out a tobacco tin and papers, and begins to roll himself a cigarette.* DAVIES *watches him.*

All them Blacks had it, Blacks, Greeks, Poles, the lot of them, that's
what, doing me out of a seat, treating me like dirt. When he come at
me tonight I told him.

> *Pause.*

15   ASTON.   Take a seat.

DAVIES.   Yes, but what I got to do first, you see, what I got to do, I got to
loosen myself up, you see what I mean? I could have got done in down
there.

> DAVIES *exclaims loudly, punches downward with closed fist, turns his back to* ASTON *and stares at the wall.*
> *Pause.* ASTON *lights a cigarette.*

ASTON.   You want to roll yourself one of these?

20   DAVIES (*turning*). What? No, no, I never smoke a cigarette. (*Pause. He comes forward.*) I'll tell you what, though. I'll have a bit of that tobacco there for my pipe, if you like.

ASTON (*handing him the tin*). Yes. Go on. Take some out of that.

DAVIES.   That's kind of you, mister. Just enough to fill my pipe, that's all.
25   (*He takes a pipe from his pocket and fills it.*) I had a tin, only . . . only a while ago. But it was knocked off. It was knocked off on the Great West Road. Where shall I put it?

ASTON.   I'll take it.

DAVIES (*handing the tin*). When he come at me tonight I told him. Didn't
30   I? You heard me tell him, didn't you?

ASTON.   I saw him have a go at you.

DAVIES.   Go at me? You wouldn't grumble. The filthy skate, an old man like me, I've had dinner with the best.

The relationship between these two characters looks uneasy. Aston, a modest but confident host, tries to make Davies feel comfortable. He searches for a chair – the previous denial of a seat a particularly sore point for Davies (ll.4–13) – sits on the bed, rolls a cigarette (S.D.), and invites his guest to do the same. Davies, however, apparently seeking refuge, betrays his insecurity through a range of garrulous self-assertions. It looks as if the colloquial character of their exchange would help ease the discomfort; but on close scrutiny their language proves to be less certain than at first sight, underlining the insecure nature of the relationship. Furthermore, Aston seems at ease in his own home while Davies anxiously frets over recent disturbances. Much, of course, will depend on the actors' readings of their parts, just as our readings – all readings – are interpretations. But from the start tone and content are played off against meaning. Davies takes Aston's 'sit down' as a friendly invitation. His own unintelligible 'Uuh. . . .' Aston takes to imply 'but where, please?'. 'Just a minute' does not mean, here, 'exactly a minute' but however long it takes Aston to find the chair; while Davies, at a loss, needs to fill up the time with talk of sit-downs (what, really, are 'good' or 'proper' ones?) and with gestures to bridge the pauses the dramatist has included in the text. Finally, 'I couldn't tell you' means 'I could'.

There is no need to continue in this vein, but it is necessary to show that the ordinary language which we take for granted is unsettled and unsettling, until sited by tone and context. Where, as seems to be the case here, the situation is itself unsure, the language only serves to aggravate the conditions it is trying to ease. Thus it is that Davies's need to say something by way of assertive protest only complicates the problems. The various grammatical irregularities of his outbursts between ll.7–13, while convincingly natural, are an ironic comment on the confidence of the racial prejudice they express. It is grimly humorous to realize that all the time he is complaining he fails to take the seat Aston offers at l.6 and again at l.15. He prefers the vague self-affirmation, 'I got to loosen myself up' (ll.16–17), the consequence of re-living the previous lines and seeing himself 'treat[ed] . . . like dirt' (l.12).

Aston's failure to respond suggests he is not really listening. All the time he is preoccupied with rolling and lighting a cigarette (S.D.s), finally inviting Davies to do the same at l.19. The following exchange resumes the lines of communication between the two which seem to have been adrift since the brief 'Sit down./Thanks.' of the start. It is as if Davies is woken from a monologue ('What?' l.20)), yet a hint of the self-assertion, the self-centredness, persists: his 'No, no, I never smoke a cigarette' is amusingly compromised by his being quick enough to take the same tobacco for his pipe (ll.21–22). The allusion to the saga of the tin 'knocked off on the Great West Road' (ll.26–27) is not only pathetically comic in its dimensions. It also reinforces the sense of uncertainty, audience and reader uncertainty, about the placing of the entire passage. We are denied the security of being put in the picture – as many playwrights are anxious to do at the start of their drama. Davies's sense of threat, presumably aggravated by his age (ll.32–33), cannot be precisely located. But when we recall that the medium of exchange in the entire piece is what we would call 'normal' language, the problem extends beyond a consideration of this particular text. Perhaps it is that most drama gives its readers and its audience a false security. Life itself denies us any sense of 'grounding' – a word we discuss in Part I – a suggestion reinforced by the use of ordinary language here, starkly dramatized by the uneasy nature of the situation.

It is as if ll.19–28 have been an interlude. At l.16 Davies just managed a 'Yes' to Aston's invitation to 'Take a seat' before retreating into himself once more, and the communication over tobacco and tins fades at l.29 as Davies takes up the story he left off at l.13. Davies's inconsistent questioning – 'Didn't I? You heard me tell him, didn't you?' (ll.29–30) – finally demands of Aston an unambiguously attentive reaction, 'I saw him have a go at you' (l.31). What we see throughout, then, as a disarming complement to lack of precise reference in the language employed, is a corresponding lack of relationship between the two who speak it. The form is dramatic, the occasion looks to be one to encourage communication, yet each character appears isolated. Davies, at the close, cannot sustain the exchange opened up by Aston's reply. As if it were inadequate, he repeats it as a question, mouths yet another colloquialism that is difficult to pin down, adds supporting details, and finally moves on to further, inconsequential self-advertisement: 'Go at me? You wouldn't grumble. The filthy skate, an old man like me, I've had dinner with the best' (ll.32–33).

We say 'as if it were inadequate', but experience of reading this passage suggests, perhaps, that it is the nature of life itself to be inadequate, or unsatisfactory. The language of everyday life provides no firm support, and communication is at best a polite effort, or the occasional meeting of self-interest. What this passage suggests is that we all muddle through on linguistic and behavioural acts of faith. What is impressive is the dramatist's outlining of this universal dilemma from such convincing psychological particulars.

(xi)

In both poems the speakers' sense of estrangement from God makes them desire redemption and harmony.

A.   *Denial*

When my devotions could not pierce
    Thy silent ears,
Then was my heart broken, as was my verse;
    My breast was full of fears
5   And disorder.

My bent thoughts, like a brittle bow,
    Did fly asunder:
Each took his way; some would to pleasures go,
    Some to the wars and thunder
10   Of alarms.

As good go anywhere, they say,
    As to benumb
Both knees and heart, in crying night and day,
    'Come, come, my God, O come!'
15   But no hearing.

O that Thou shouldst give dust a tongue
    To cry to Thee,
And then not hear it crying! all day long
    My heart was in my knee,
20   But no hearing.

Therefore my soul lay out of sight,
    Untuned, unstrung:
My feeble spirit, unable to look right,
    Like a nipt blossom, hung
25   Discontented.

O cheer and tune my heartless breast,
    Defer no time;
That so Thy favours granting my request,
    They and my mind may chime,
30   And mend my rhyme.

B.   *A Better Resurrection*

I have no wit, no words, no tears;
    My heart within me like a stone
Is numbed too much for hopes or fears.
    Look right, look left, I dwell alone;

56

5   I lift mine eyes, but dimmed with grief
       No everlasting hills I see;
    My life is in the falling leaf:
       O Jesus, quicken me.

    My life is like a faded leaf,
10   My harvest dwindled to a husk:
    Truly my life is void and brief
       And tedious in the barren dusk;
    My life is like a frozen thing,
       No bud nor greenness can I see;
15   Yet rise it shall — the sap of Spring;
       O Jesus, rise in me.

    My life is like a broken bowl,
       A broken bowl that cannot hold
    One drop of water for my soul
20   Or cordial in the searching cold;
    Cast in the fire the perished thing;
       Melt and remould it, till it be
    A royal cup for Him, my King:
       O Jesus, drink of me.

In declaiming anxieties about lack of spiritual security, the speaker in poem A seems much the more vigorous of the two. The irregular lines, with their frequent interruptions, create a dramatic tone, addressed directly to God Himself throughout. The speaker's complaint in poem B of complete dejection is conveyed in regular stanzas, only calling on Jesus specifically to effect a remedy at the end of each. Both poems, however, suggest a direct connection between a state of grace – or lack of it – and the ability to write poetry. The 'verse' of poem A is actually 'broken' by the way that word dislocates the rhythm of l.3 – the sudden trochaic foot disturbs the iambic stress pattern, which makes the line-break, or caesura, stronger than the comma would otherwise imply. Despair dictates the language of ll.13–14, 'crying night and day, / "Come, come, my God, O come!" ', which is echoed in the next stanza, while the 'untuned, unstrung' of l.22 reinforces the connection between spiritual and poetic discord. A final plea for God to restore harmony, and thus the speaker's 'rhyme', brings the poem to a close. Paradoxically, then, this is a poem which elaborates upon the inability to write poetry because of an absence of spiritual equilibrium. It might be difficult for a modern reader to sympathize personally with the religious anxieties of the past, but he or she might well query whether anyone in a supposed state of spiritual peril should be capable of the control, the resources necessary to write poetry. This speaker actually exploits this dilemma to create the poem.

It looks as if the same will apply in poem B. The speaker announces a lack of all the ingredients necessary for poetry, and then proceeds to three stanzas involving them all. 'I have no wit', which means shaping imagination or intelligence, as well as wittiness or light-heartedness. Thus 'no words' arise, and 'no tears', no emotional vitality, even if of an unhappy kind. But 'words' evidently follow in which the reader finds all these qualities, even if the tone is generally passive. The contradiction, then, pinpoints the dilemma built into poem A. You write about the impossibility of writing in order to emphasize your condition, but poem B makes no more use of the paradox after its first line. In example (vi) in this section we have more to say about the way writers treat the relationship between experience and its expression. The situation in that passage is so disabling that the characters are at a loss to describe it. However there, as here, we are prompted to reflect how writers use language like 'words cannot express . . .' in order to lend weight to their subsequent contradictions.

In viewing the speaker's life repeatedly and variously in terms of images of natural decay, emptiness, and immobility, poem B intensifies its mood of hopelessness in language which is at once understandable and familiar. 'My life is in the falling leaf' (l.7), for example – not just 'like the falling leaf', which would lessen the sense of identification – like a faded leaf' (l.9), 'like a frozen thing' (l.13), with 'searching cold' (l.20), and achievements or potential unrealized, 'harvest dwindled to a husk' (l.10). While Spring will renew the natural world (ll.14–15) the speaker feels condemned to decay, for 'no everlasting hills' (l.6) are visible. You are unlikely to know that this is a reference to *Psalm* 121, where, by contrast, the lifting up of eyes to the hills leads to a sense of God's support, but the feeling of a lack of eternal renewal is quite clear, which results in 'life [being] void' (l.11), meaning both empty and invalid. But although there is more sense of striving in poem A, both speakers realize that it is necessary to call upon God to do all the work of redemption. This is confessed accusingly in stanzas three and four of poem A, with a more conciliatory tone adopted in the last. Jesus is appealed to with increasing intensity at the end of each stanza in poem B, to grant the speaker that sap of spiritual renewal which is the promise of His springtime resurrection (alluded to in ll.15–16). This supplication reaches its highest strain in the last stanza. The natural images give way to life being compared to a 'broken bowl', whose wholesale repair is strenuously demanded of Christ in a series of imperatives, 'cast', 'melt', and 'remould', so the speaker might be thrust into the 'fire' not of hell but of renewal. This seems to be a clear reference to Christ's most significant pact with frail humanity, symbolized in the cup of Communion, but so forceful is the desire to be saved that the last line insists that Christ 'drink of [the speaker]' rather than the other way round. As in poem A, the speaker feels that salvation depends upon

God's grace, and, although it is not a question of God helping those who help themselves, the reader feels that the climax brings a measure of satisfaction and relief if only because of the strength of voice with which that grace is demanded.

Poem A, by contrast, actively seeks renewal through 'devotions', but from the start both God and the reader are left in no doubt where the fault is made to lie – with God's 'silent ears' (l.2). The point is re-emphasized by the refrain 'But no hearing' at the close of stanzas three and four, and used to excuse the pursuit of 'pleasures' and 'wars' touched on in stanza two. By stanza five, however, the speaker's spiritual condition, 'like a nipt blossom', has more in common with the prevailing mood and imagery of poem B. In poem A, though, the cry for redemption from despair is impertinent, for it accuses God of denying the very thing He grants to penitent mankind – mercy. What this results in is a much more energetic style of writing than in poem B. The alternating long and short lines are abruptly broken, as exemplified earlier with l.3, or the sense reinforced by splitting rhythms and clauses between one line and the next, as at ll.24–25, 'hung/Discontented', where the impact of the one-word line is added to by inversion of stress, the main emphasis coming on the first syllable. Another telling example occurs at ll.21–22. Overall the language is direct, emphatic, playing off strong consonants against the vowel sounds, with the further effect of alliteration, as in l.6, 'My bent thoughts, like a brittle bow'.

The irony is, however, that the more the speaker complains with self-justifying vigour, the more he or she reinforces the estrangement for which relief is sought. There is no accusing voice in poem B, but here the speaker needs to 'cheer and tune [his or her] heartless breast' (l.26) out of discordant railings at that very God of whom salvation is wished. Only then might He bestow his 'favours' (l.28). Whether God's grace be earned or entirely given with no strings attached is a problem which has exercised Christians throughout the ages, with no resolution either way. If earned, you compromise God's independence – He is then obliged to give it to you. If God-given regardless, it means that your behaviour, for good or ill, counts for nothing. What is certain is that frail humanity has always called upon God in a variety of ways and moods, and both these poems highlight the problems involved. The ironies which the reader sees to be at the speaker's expense in poem A suggest that the poet who conceived of them, as distinct from the speaker he or she has created, knows where the faults lie. Otherwise we should have to conclude that the poet did not appreciate the implications of his or her own writing. The tone in poem B is more straight-forward, but we must be careful not to identify the speaker with the poet. Poets speak through 'personae': the voice is sited in a dramatic work of art at some complex remove from the poet in his or her own person. It is dangerous to see any kind of poetry as an uncomplicated confessional.

The irony in poem A is sustained, for example, into the last stanza. 'Defer no time' (l.27) means 'do not postpone the occasion of your relief' and 'do not defer, make concessions at any time' if this speaker should continue to be as ungracious as he or she has been earlier in the poem. Yet there is a sense of contrition. The penultimate stanza tells of the results of going about things wrongly, before the submission of the last. 'Defer no time' also refers to the relationship between poetry and mood: 'time', harmony, will be restored to 'rhyme' when 'mind' itself is 'mend[ed]'. The trochaic rhythms of the last lines of stanzas 1–5 give way in the sixth to a regular iambic pattern, in a rhyming couplet, 'chime,/ . . . rhyme', whereas the preceding last lines were unrhymed, unresolved – indeed 'hung/Discontented' (ll.24–25). The first stanza tells of the loss of poetic harmony when God seemed distant. Its restoration at the close anticipates a reconciliation.

Unlike the speaker in poem B, the speaker in poem A advertises and sustains the rôle of poet throughout. The fact that his or her art is apparently harmed by despair helps explain the strenuous nature of the complaints. But it is only apparently harmed: we are back to the paradox mentioned earlier because the speaker's condition gives rise to the vigorous art of this poem. In a larger sense it is often conflict, seemingly destructive of the powers of expression, which is made to result in compelling writing. The speaker of poem A is supposedly in the same position at the start as the speaker of poem B in having 'no wit, no words', but plenty of 'tears', which are not enough without the controlling qualities of the other two. Then both speakers create poems, with all the essential ingredients, out of apparent poetic dead-ends – like, as we said earlier, the familiar 'words cannot express' as a prelude to effective writing or ambitious subject-matter.

The following extract from a twentieth-century novel describes a young woman's reactions to an erotic encounter.

Love? It is an absolute fact that the name of 'love' did not in the first eternal moments even occur to her. And when it did she gave it but little importance. She had to admit that she had not consciously thought of George Cannon with love — at any rate with love as she had imagined
5   love to be. Indeed, her immediate experience would not fit any theory that she could formulate. But with the inexorable realism of her sex she easily dismissed inconvenient names and theories, and accommodated herself to the fact. And the fact was that she overwhelmingly wanted George Cannon, and, as she now recognized, had wanted him ever since
10 she first saw him. The recognition afforded her intense pleasure. She abandoned herself candidly to this luxury of an unknown desire. It was incomparably the most splendid and dangerous experience that she had ever had. She did not reason, and she had no wish to reason. She was set above reason. Happy to the point of delicious pain, she yet yearned
15 forward to a happiness far more excruciating. She was perfectly aware that her bliss would be torment until George Cannon had married her, until she had wholly surrendered to him.

Yet at intervals a voice said very clearly within her: 'All this is wrong. This is base and shameful. This is something to blush for, really!' She did
20 blush. But her blushes were a part of the delight. And the voice was not persistent. She could silence it with scarcely an effort, despite its clarity.

'Kiss me!' George Cannon demanded of her, with eager masterfulness.

The request shocked her for an instant, and the young girl in her was about to revolt. But she kissed him — an act which combined the sweet-
25 ness of submission with the glory of triumph! She looked at him steadily, confident in herself and in him. She felt that he knew how to love. His emotion filled her with superb pride. She seemed to be saying to him in a doomed rapture: 'Do you think I don't know what I am doing? I know! I know!'

30 The current of the river was tremendous. She foresaw the probability of disaster. She was aware that she had definitely challenged the hazard of fate. But she was not terrified in the dark, swirling night of her destiny. She straightened her shoulders. With all her innocence and ignorance and impulsiveness and weakness, she had behind her the unique and
35 priceless force of her youth. She was young, and she put her trust in life.

In thirty-five lines of prose describing what is clearly an important stage in the novel, there are only two words actually spoken. These are given to the male character, George Cannon, and take the form of an imperative, 'Kiss me', whose commanding tone the novelist further emphasizes by an exclamation mark, the verb 'demanded' (instead of the flatter, more usual, narrative word 'said') and the adverbial phrase, 'with eager masterfulness' (l.22). In terms of action, then, the scene looks to be operating according to the gender stereotypes of assertive male and silent, passive female.

There are other elements in the text which seem to confirm this sexual polarization. The young woman recognizes not only that she wants George, but that she 'had wanted him ever since she first saw him' (ll.9–10). This acknowledgement is a source of 'intense pleasure' (l.10) for her; and she abandons herself to her desire for him, looking forward to a complete surrender (ll.10–11, 17). All this accords with common assumptions about female sexuality: desire for the male is naturally evoked by first sight (even if this is only retrospectively acknowledged, there is no doubting its truth), and the rôle of the woman is to yield herself to the man. The command, 'Kiss me', thus acts as a spoken demonstration of an unspoken relationship. The lines of sexual politics are clearly drawn up.

Is the novelist confirming these assumptions in his or her own voice? It is the novelist, of course, who is setting the scene and its implications; and it is the novelist who, perhaps condescendingly, talks of 'the inexorable realism of her sex' (l.6). The phrase certainly distances the novelist's tone from identification with the woman. Although it is perfectly possible that a female writer might be doing this, the likely inference does seem to be that the novelist's attitudes are those of a man with conventional assumptions about female sexuality.

But there are some complicating factors. One is that the novelist does not seem to be interested in George himself. The phrase, 'with eager masterfulness', is the only clue we have to his feelings, the narrative being almost entirely concentrated on the woman's responses. The reader thus sees the scene from her point of view, not in the sense that one character controls the narrative (as in passage (i) and (v)), but because the novelist fixes attention upon her, making the male character very much an external figure. It may be that the structure confirms further sexual stereotypes, those of the sensitive, emotional woman and the mysterious, unknowable man. It could, however, be that the entire novel is really concerned with the female character, George being relatively unimportant. Evidence for the latter interpretation may be found in the extent to which this love-scene is, for her, placed within a larger time-scale. Her past is implied in the reference to first seeing George; but her future is, more significantly, anticipated in terms which accord her an active consciousness: 'She foresaw the probability of disaster. She was aware that she had definitely challenged the hazard of fate' (ll.30–32). The words the novelist uses for her future may be vague ('the dark, swirling night of her destiny', l.32), perhaps reflecting uncertainty within the rather sensational language, but her self-awareness is made to be very sharp and precise: disaster she sees as not just possible, but probable, and she takes her chance with open eyes.

Although some of the language places the woman in a passive position, her self-control and confidence are equally emphasized. There are examples in the first paragraph, where the language of 'she abandoned herself' and the negative phrasing of 'She did not reason' (l.13) – conforming to the conventional view of female irrationality? – are matched by 'She was perfectly aware' (l.15) and 'She had no wish to reason' (l.13). Thus she, paradoxically, is conscious of her emotional state and voluntarily sets reason aside. After the kiss, her self-awareness is even more marked. She looks 'steadily' at him, she is 'confident' (of herself as well as of him as a lover), she is proud, her inner voice speaks of knowing what she is doing, and she is 'aware' (ll.25–31).

It may be that the co-existence of these two attitudes reflects confusion in the novelist's presentation of her. But it may also be the case that the writer is portraying a woman who is both self-assured and undergoing a powerful and new experience. The sexual element in her feelings is throughout strongly emphasized. The passage begins by questioning the nature of her feelings, distinguishing between what 'she had imagined love to be' and the reality of 'her immediate experience' (ll.4–5). The novelist here is contrasting her preconceptions – more stereotypes – with the real thing, thereby claiming convincing status for prose in an area which is frequently marred by conventional language. The novelist's realism echoes the truth of her erotic feelings: she 'overwhelmingly wanted' (l.8) George, her emotions are of both 'pleasure' and 'desire' (ll.10–11), and her surrender is juxtaposed to her potential marriage to him ('until George Cannon had married her, until she had wholly surrendered to him', ll.16–17). In the final paragraph, her youth is both a cause of her 'innocence and ignorance . . . and weakness' (ll.33–34) and of her confidence ('she put her trust in life', l.35).

This division within the character is further indicated by the novelist's extensive use of the rhetorical device of oxymoron, in which apparently contradictory terms are brought together, often as adjective and noun. So the woman is happy to the point of 'delicious pain' (l.14), she yearns for a 'happiness far more excruciating' (l.15), her current state of 'bliss would be torment' (l.16) until the moment of surrender, and her conscious acceptance of surrender – the active decision to be passive – is expressed in a 'doomed rapture' (l.28). Tensions are found elsewhere in the narrative, as when the voice of the woman's conscience is said to be both clear and easily silenced, and her blushing for shame is actually a part of her pleasure (ll.20–21). This is most in evidence at the text's one moment of action: the kiss is described as combining 'the sweetness of submission with the glory of triumph' (ll.24–25), a phrase whose first term accords with a stereotypical view of female passiveness but whose second grants her a dominant rôle.

The novelist's provision of all this information about the woman contrasts with the lack of exchange between the two characters themselves. Our intimate knowledge of her is not shared by George; while George himself remains very much an unknown quantity. The writer's decision to focus so completely on the woman's feelings would seem to support the view that the tensions in her experience are part of a more extensive analysis of the growing-up of a young woman. It is certainly her powerful and mixed emotions which are the novelist's central interest, thus explaining the unequal distribution within the narrative.

The following sonnet takes the form of a private meditation in a grave-yard.

Sonnet Written in the Church Yard at Middleton in Sussex

Pressed by the moon, mute arbitress of tides,
While the loud equinox its power combines,
The sea no more its swelling surge confines,
But o'er the shrinking land sublimely rides.
5 The wild blast, rising from the western cave,
Drives the huge billows from their heaving bed,
Tears from their grassy tombs the village dead,
And breaks the silent sabbath of the grave!
With shells and sea-weed mingled, on the shore
10 Lo! their bones whiten in the frequent wave;
But vain to them the winds and waters rave;
They hear the warring elements no more:
While I am doomed — by life's long storm oppressed,
To gaze with envy on their gloomy rest.

The title of this poem, at once precise and elaborate, does more than locate it geographically: 'sonnet' sets it in a formal literary tradition, and 'Written in the Church Yard' relates it to one of the most famous poems in the English language, Thomas Gray's 'Elegy Written in a Country Church-Yard' (1751). Without more information, we must be careful about drawing further inferences. For example, we cannot consider whether or not it might be influenced by, or be an influence on, Gray's elegy. The present exercise does not, in any case, necessarily involve such comparisons, and, although a student at this level might have heard of the Gray poem, a detailed knowledge of it will not be assumed. An analysis of the sonnet which makes no reference to the 'Elegy' will, therefore, be entirely valid. This is, however, an instance where the maxim that the more you have read, the more you will gain from literature, is particularly appropriate; for a response to the text which was able to discuss the extent to which elegy as a *genre* focuses upon the actual graves of the dead (ll.7–8) or upon the poet's own situation (ll.13–14) would present an illuminating breadth of sophistication.

However, an analysis which took as its starting-point the nature of a sonnet could be equally revealing. An awareness of the form and history of the sonnet in English is the kind of 'technical' knowledge which, when creatively applied to the particular example we are discussing, can provide the basis for productive inquiry. Here the poem's punctuation and rhyme-scheme place it within one of the most familiar English sonnet-structures, that which operates in three sets of four lines together with a concluding couplet. The most usual form of this – largely because of Shakespeare's use of it – has the four lines rhyming alternately (a b a b). Although our example's a b b a rhyme-scheme (with the further variation that the 'a' rhyme in the second quatrain is the same as the 'b' rhyme in the third) differs from this pattern, it still serves the customary function of marking out clear stages in the poem's argument. The opening sentence describes the power of the sea; the next four lines narrate the effect of the storm upon the graveyard; ll.9–12 contrast that effect with the dead's unawareness of what is happening to their remains; and the couplet defines the poet's own direct responses.

By virtue of its pointed, epigrammatic quality, the couplet in such sonnets is often the stage to which the rest of the poem builds, its 'punch-line'. This certainly seems to be true here, for the couplet's combination of comparison and contrast with what has gone before makes it both a conclusion to the poem's argument and a striking statement. The comparison lies principally in the way in which the literal storm, the 'wild blast' (l.5), that occupies the poem's central section, is applied metaphorically to the buffetings of life in general. The contrast lies principally in the change to the first-person, prepared for by the poet's emphatic italicization of '*They*' in l.12 and the colon at the end of the line, which leads the reader to expect either an illustration or – as in this case – an antithesis. (Contrast the full-stop and exclamation mark which end lines 1–4 and 5–8 respectively.) The '*They*/I' opposition forms its own structure within the larger shape of the sonnet. Although both poet and dead suffer storms, the former's own perception is set against their ignorance. So what looks at first to be their deprivation ('vain to them', l.11) turns instead into their advantage. It is the living writer's knowledge of life which leads him or her to prefer ('gaze with envy', l.14) their unconsciousness to the doom of consciousness.

The sonnet, then, attempts to express the pain of human awareness. So it is significant that, even in the descriptive parts of the poem, the writer has tended to perceive the scene in human terms, thus further connecting the elements of the poem's argument. The first four lines divide neatly into two of cause and two of effect: it is the power of the moon to affect tides, allied to the tradition of equinoctial gales (which are supposed to be particularly common at the autumnal equinox), which makes the sea so high as to encroach on the land, making it shrink as it is invaded. In this description, both the moon ('mute arbitress of tides', l.1: the moon is traditionally seen as feminine, classical mythology linking it to the unchanging realm of the Goddesses Cynthia and Diana, while all beneath is transient) and the sea ('rides', l.4) are given human attributes. The destructive power of the storm, described in lines 5–8 as so disturbing the 'grassy tombs' of 'the village dead', is then appropriately energized by means of verbs – one per line – whose meaning can easily be related to human actions ('rising', 'Drives', 'Tears', 'breaks'). The middle two verbs are given added force by being placed strongly at the beginning of lines, so reversing the more usual iambic rhythm of English verse ('Drives the . . .', 'Tears from . . .'). Normal rhythm is restored in the last verb of the sequence ('And breaks . . .'), so that the sentence comes to rest in a regular iambic line even as the dead villagers' rest ('sabbath' etymologically denoting what we refer to in our phrase, 'day of rest') is broken.

This rhythmic energy contributes to the violence of the scene which is conveyed by the poet's choice of language. But there is a problem for the reader's response here. For the language used ('swelling surge', 'wild blast', 'heaving bed', 'Tears', 'breaks', 'rave') may strike us as extravagant and sensational, matching the grotesque nature of the event. Is the poem's treatment of its subject melodramatic? How feasible is it for us to take the event as realistic rather than an increasingly exaggerated stage-effect? Perhaps the tenth line, with its forced exclamation to witness bones being bleached by salt-water, is the most difficult for us to take entirely seriously. Are we dangerously close to the world of horror film?

If we do respond in this way, then it is the poem's attempt to present the writer's private sorrow that is doomed. We cannot be expected to take that emotion seriously if the earlier sections of the sonnet are forced and unconvincing. Sincerity, as we noted in Part I, is, as far as literary expression is concerned, created by style rather than intention. No matter how true or false the feelings of the poet were at the time of composition, it is the poem's language which conveys, or fails to convey, emotion. In judging the effectiveness of the language here, a further problem should make us qualify our initial reactions. The language of sincerity depends upon assumptions which may differ from age to age, from region to region, even from class to class. So a form of language which was perfectly acceptable as a register of emotion at a past time might, because of its strangeness to us, strike an unconvincing note. Recognizing this will not change our responses, but it will make our estimation of their validity more cautious. Here, again, extensive literary experience is of immense value: to have read other poems of this type would provide us with a wider context for the appreciation of this poem.

The issue of effective expression of feeling is particularly important in a poem which attempts to define strong personal emotion. If the sea is 'Pressed' (l.1: again, the verb is emphasized by its forceful rhythmic position), the poet is 'oppressed' (l.13) by the storm of life. The couplet's rhyme, bringing together 'oppressed' and 'rest', sets in final counterpoint the 'silent sabbath' of the dead and the poet's living consciousness. Whether that consciousness expresses itself in terms which are truly or falsely emotive remains the central question.

(xiv)

Passage A describes the environment and life of an industrial town.
Passage B relates a young man's gaining his first job in a factory.

A.   It was a town of red brick, or of brick that would have been red if the
smoke and ashes had allowed it; but, as matters stood, it was a town of
unnatural red and black, like the painted face of a savage. It was a town
of machinery and tall chimneys, out of which interminable serpents of
5 smoke trailed themselves for ever and ever, and never got uncoiled. It
had a black canal in it, and a river that ran purple with ill-smelling dye, and
vast piles of building full of windows where there was a rattling and a
trembling all day long, and where the piston of the steam engine
worked monotonously up and down, like the head of an elephant in a
10 state of melancholy madness. It contained several large streets all very
like one another, and many small streets still more like one another,
inhabited by people equally like one another, who all went in and out at
the same hours, with the same sound upon the same pavements, to do
the same work, and to whom every day was the same as yesterday and
15 tomorrow, and every year the counterpart of the last and the next.

B.   Ted grunted: 'Washer name?'
'Harry Hardcastle, sir.'
'Six o'clock t'morrer mornin'. . . . Machine shop, think on . . .' He
cocked a glance at Harry's clothes: 'An see y' come in a pair overalls.
5 This ain't a bloody school.'
Harry blushed: 'Yes, sir,' he mumbled, meekly.
'All right. Muck off. . . . Don't hang around here. Hey! Here, tek these
here papers. Get y'r owld man t' fill 'em up. An' y' bloody clockin'-on
number's,' glancing at a chart: '2510. Clock number fourteen. Clock on
10 o' mornin' an' clock off o' night. *Don't* clock at dinner. Think on, now,
don't you go'n make a muck of it like all t'others do, the dense lot o'
bastards,' jerking his thumb: "Oppit, now, 'oppit, 'oppit, 'oppit.' Confused with excitement, Harry made himself scarce. What luck! He really
was engaged. And in so short a space of time! What would the boys
15 have to say to this? He gazed at the papers in his hand. There was the
magic word 'Indentures!' And they'd given him a number, 2510. There
was the hallmark of his engagement. Better make a note of it. He wrote it
on a corner of the indenture.
The man with the badge in his coat again intercepted him. Harry told
20 him of his success: 'All right, clear off, now, until tomorrow,' the man
said, not unkindly: 'Can't have y' hangin' about here.'
He went outside the gates thrilled, spirits soaring, paused and turned
to survey the great place, enthralled as a child in a Christmas toy
shop.

One of the many striking features of passage A is the use of the impersonal pronoun at the beginning of each of its four sentences. This amounts to an insistent and contemptuous denial of a name to the town in question, reinforcing the depersonalizing effects 'it' has upon its population, both in terms of work and surroundings. A contributory factor is the inescapable monotony of existence, the impression of which reaches a climax in the rhythmic and verbal repetitions of the last sentence, where the reiteration of 'same' five times emphatically precludes that variety of adjectives we might otherwise anticipate to describe the differences of the daily round.

But it is not that the images which the narrative employs are commonplace. Far from it – they are as startling in their singularity as the verbal effects are in their repetitiveness. The perspectives of one image strengthen the effects of another until the cumulative effect suggests at one and the same time a town of distinctive feature, and one that is characteristic of all others of its kind. 'It' is both particular and general, which extends the range of the passage's forceful criticism. The description of the town as one of 'red brick' is immediately qualified by the 'smoke and ashes' which gave it the appearance of 'the painted face of a savage' (ll.1–3). This strongly indicates the barbaric nature of what, from a different point of view, might be seen to be the civilized character of the industrial landscape. The pistons of the town's machinery, 'work-[ing] monotonously up and down, like the head of an elephant in a state of melancholy madness' (ll.9–10), extend the idea of savagery to a jungle where the mechanical parts seem to reflect the despair of those who have to work them. The vistas of both images expand and echo those created by the verbal patterns – the brutality of the environment and the relentless workings of vast machinery creating a corresponding inhumanity and enormous frustration in the rhythms of life forced upon the town's trapped inhabitants. The similes might seem excessive, but they are related to what passes for factual description, underlining the point that exaggeration in these surroundings is hardly possible. The colours of canal and river, full of filth and dye, while giving some general idea of the manufacture, also reflect the blacks and reds of the 'painted face of a savage'. The rattling and trembling of 'vast piles of building full of windows' is the result of the frenzied working of the elephantine machinery (ll.7–10). These 'vast piles' also prepare the ground for the undifferentiated mass of humanity which works within it. They lead the passage to the pile-driving 'up and down' locomotion of vast engines, which in its turn anticipates the 'in and out' (l.12) monotony of daily existence. The serpentine metaphor for the smoke which 'trailed [itself] for ever and ever, and never got uncoiled' (ll.4–5) both continues the jungle theme and sustains our focus upon the suffocating and imprisoning existence of those in its grip beneath. Throughout, then, the narrative survey possesses a remarkable cohesion.

There is a hint, also, of the unchristian brutality of it all. The Satanic serpent presides over the scene, while 'a river that ran purple with ill-smelling dye' (l.6) looks like a reminder of the first plague of Egypt, where God turned the river into blood so that it stank and all the fish died, because Pharaoh would not release the Israelites. Or the writer might expect the reader to recall the last plagues in *Revelation*, where God's wrath is poured in vials upon the Earth so that all rivers and seas turn to blood. In this broad perspective the whole scene becomes the vicious inheritance of evil mankind ripe for God's judgement. The verbal and rhythmic build-up to the climax of the last lines suggests, perhaps, grotesque parodies of God's 'world without end. Amen', echoed in the final blessing at church service and at the conclusion to the Lord's Prayer. God's kingdom on earth has been eclipsed by never-ending enslavement. The narrator has made a sweep through the landscape to emphasize that the collective birth-right has been sold to the industrial devil.

By contrast, passage B concentrates upon individuals, with the industrial scene as backdrop. Rather than conveying universal despair through a bold and broad narrative overview, passage B treats of a young man's excitement at the prospect of gaining adult status through the change from school to factory work. Details are focused in dialogue (ll.1–12, 20–21) and dramatized glimpses into his thoughts and feelings (ll.12–18), with further description of these in the final short paragraph. It looks, then, as if both style and mood are in marked contrast to those of passage A. The rehearsal of factory rules leaves no room for daring images and elaborate verbal patternings. While Ted's vulgar language suggests that Harry Hardcastle's calling him 'sir' (ll.2, 6) is out of place, his respect does hint at the importance and approval he attaches to a life-style which he sees as full of promise, and which, in general terms, is so forcefully and dramatically censured in passage A. Harry keeps his thoughts to himself, for it would be impossible for him to communicate the nature of them to the older man.

Whereas the narrator of passage A sees the industrial population collectively chained to its dehumanizing existence, Harry eagerly gazes on the 'magic word "Indentures!" ' (l.16) – his binding apprenticeship which he sees as the irreversible sign of real identity, the freedom and prestige of male adulthood ('What would the boys have to say to this?', ll.14–15). Even the monotony of clocking on and clocking off, which reminds the worker every day that his life and time are not his own, is looked forward to keenly. The anonymity of his 'number, 2510' (l.16), which he thinks of as a personal symbol of achievement, in reality reduces him to one of that mass whose relentless existence has been so powerfully drawn in passage A.

The irony is that his excitement highlights the very boyishness he is so understandably eager to get rid of. Apprenticeships are supposed to confer security and prospects, but Harry seems at least as much concerned with their status in other ways. He might carry credit with other boys, but in the workshop he will find himself very much the junior. This is anticipated in Ted's general tone of language towards him; but in putting him in his place (' "this ain't a bloody school." Harry blushed', ll.5–6), Ted does signal nonetheless the all-important change from classroom to factory floor. Equally his general assertiveness does suggest a world of male cut-and-thrust from which Harry has so far been excluded; but the sense of disgruntlement, conveyed in clipped dialect and slang, indicates at the same time the brutalizing effect of the workplace, in contrast to Harry's own manner, if not his expectations. It is significant that the kindly dismissal Harry receives from the second, unnamed man (ll.20–21) is kept to a minimum so as not to disturb the balance between Harry's enthusiasm and Ted's own aggressive cynicism. Clocking on and off, for the latter, provides an opportunity indiscriminately to slate 'all t' others . . . the dense lot o' bastards' who supposedly 'make a muck of it' (ll.11–12). It reminds us very much of the manner of Davies in the first part of example (x); but, more to the point here, the stark lack of humanity echoes in a less colourful way the general message of passage A.

In this light the last paragraph must also be read ironically. 'Outside the gates' the boy's spirits soar – not as they would for those inside at the temporary release on Friday night, nor because he is outside enjoying his last day of freedom, but because tomorrow he will be inside until the day he retires. The last image of him, as he 'survey[s] the great place, enthralled as a child in a Christmas toy shop' (ll.23–24), fittingly highlights the illusory and childlike nature of his expectations. The simile works two ways: there will be little good will in the world he is about to enter, although 'in a Christmas toy shop' beyond the gates he might enjoy a very modest degree of purchasing power. However, the play upon 'enthralled', meaning both 'charmed' and 'enslaved', suggests that his loss of liberty is an insidiously high price to pay, and reminds us of the depiction of inescapable confinement under 'interminable serpents of smoke' in passage A.

Through clever management of striking images and verbal effects, passage A presents a clear-cut indictment of the industrial scene. Its overview of one town has general relevance for all, and sees the industrial inheritance in the broadest terms of good and evil. Passage B lacks these resonances, but has compensating subtleties in the way it is structured. It offers an individualized point of view which anticipates much promise from the factory environment, only to undermine it by playing it off against the dispiriting perspectives which Ted, an experienced hand, affords. From this emerge passage B's larger implications about the change from boy to man and the consequent loss of freedom in the need to earn a living. Both passages, apparently taken from novels, can be seen as critiques of what Marx calls the capitalist economy – where man is obliged to sell the one commodity he possesses, his labour, in order to survive at a level which annihilates meaningful existence (passage A) or seriously compromises it (passage B).

(xv)

Both the following texts reflect on the First World War. The prose text is an extract from an autobiography.

A. *In Memoriam (Easter 1915)*

> The flowers left thick at nightfall in the wood
> This Eastertide call into mind the men,
> Now far from home, who, with their sweethearts, should
> Have gathered them and will do never again.

B. My bullet wound had healed quickly. A couple of weeks in a London
hospital had been followed by a month's convalescence in perfect surroundings, for I was one of several officers who were staying with Lord
and Lady Brassey at their beautiful home in Sussex. All possible kind-
5 ness had been showered on me, every opportunity was there for
healthy contentment and mental relaxation, and the fine early summer
weather made the place an earthly paradise. But somehow or other I had
only achieved superficial felicity, for the contrast between this luxurious
and delightful existence and my lurid experiences on the Arras battle-
10 field had been with me all the time. My mind had dwelt continually on the
battalion with which I had been serving. Since I left it, ten officers had
been killed and fourteen wounded. It wasn't surprising that this undermined my complacency about my own good fortune. There were
moments when I felt irrationally hostile to the graciously-organized
15 amenities of Chapelwood Manor which were providing such superlative
compensation for my brief participation in the Spring Offensive. While in
France, my anti-war ideas had been in abeyance. Out there one had
been too busy to ask the reason why. One couldn't be 'above the battle'
while engaged in it, and I had sometimes been able to resort to the
20 emotional 'happy warrior' attitude which was so helpful in sustaining
one's fortitude.

The poem has a directness and simplicity appropriate to the nature of an epitaph, which its title ('in memory') declares it to be. The language used is uncomplicated, and the rhyme-scheme (a b a b) is a common one for poems composed in four-line units. But the parenthesis in the title alerts us to the fact that this is not a conventional epitaph for a named person. The dead are many, and retain the obscurity of anonymity. They are also absent, departed geographically as well as in death. The comforting language of home ('sweethearts', l.3) and its cosily rural customs (gathering flowers at Eastertide) are placed against their opposite: the men are 'far from home' (l.3), and it is they who have been gathered by death. The Easter setting provides an ironic basis for the poem, because the time when Christ's resurrection is celebrated provides no return for the dead soldiers: the phrase 'never again' (l.4), significantly rhyming with 'the men' (l.2), concludes the poem with unqualified finality.

It is possible, however, to detect some confusion of thought within this apparently clear-cut structure. If flowers can be allowed to 'call into mind' (l.2), they do so because the men who should have picked them are no longer there to do so. An analogy seems to be suggested between the flowers being 'left thick at nightfall' (l.1) and the dead soldiers fallen into the darkness of death. But these flowers are still living precisely because the men have not gathered them: thus the analogy is between living flowers and dead men. An escape from a charge of logical inconsistency might be found by seeing the relationship between flowers and soldiers as contrast rather than analogy, the poem ironically perceiving that living flowers are a memorial for dead humanity. On Remembrance Day we have to be content with wreaths.

Whatever our interpretation of this point, the poet's attitude seems one of straightforward lament. Any hint of criticism of the circumstances leading to the men's absence can only, perhaps, be located in the emphatic placing of 'should' at the end of the third line. If the soldiers 'ought to' have gathered the flowers, then there is a sense of the natural rightness (again ironic, since gathering flowers destroys them) having been disrupted. But there is no further definition of attitude and, indeed, were it not for the title, we would not know that the poem is about the First World War.

The prose passage, by contrast, is very specific in its First World War setting, and much more open in its point of view. Just as in the poem, home (London, Sussex) is set against absence of home (Arras, France); but the writer's geographical precision here goes along with a far more realized presentation of both. The author has direct experience of home and abroad, the bullet wound suffered in one being the cause of a more pleasant time spent recuperating in the other. Hence the passage can particularize both. In France, ten officers have been killed and fourteen wounded since he left (ll.11–12), an indication of the rapidity of casualties at the front. The writer describes his experiences technically (a 'Spring Offensive' on the 'Arras battlefield', ll.16, 9–10) and emotively ('lurid', l.9). Back in England, he again identifies place (Chapelwood Manor in Sussex), while providing appropriate atmosphere by mentioning 'fine early summer weather' (ll.6–7) and by describing his surroundings as 'perfect' (l.2), 'beautiful' (l.4), an 'earthly paradise' (l.7).

In further contrast with the poem, this precision is used as a means of developing implied criticism. The home he is staying in is an aristocratic one ('Lord and Lady Brassey', ll.3–4) where officers can stay in comfort. Where, the reader might wonder, do other ranks go for their convalescence? Dead men, whether officers or not, cannot, of course, recover at all. The comfort of these people at home furnishes a telling contrast to conditions at the battle-front, and, if this is Lord and Lady Brassey's contribution to the war effort, it is a somewhat uneasy one. The disparity now is more than a cause for lament: it is, implicity, a politically engaged distinction by the writer. The Lord and Lady Brasseys possess the 'England, home and beauty' promoted by First World War propagandists. They look after the wounded representatives of an officer class which is involved in a war fought to preserve their way of life.

There is a problem in assessing responses to an emotive subject like war. It is impossible to be unaware of a conflict of attitudes between art which glorifies war and art which depicts war as unpleasant and futile. The latter viewpoint has particularly emerged from First World War experience, reflecting a general perception of the senselessness of the conflict. *All Quiet on the Western Front, Oh What a Lovely War* and the poetry of Wilfred Owen have largely established a consensus about this war, if not about all wars. We do, therefore, have to guard against preconceptions, against coming to texts like these with ready-made ideas, seeking their confirmation in what we read.

So to make too much of the significance of 'should' in the poem would be to be tempted into too precise a reading. We are not justified in seeing specific protest in a text which is general in its statements. The generality extends to the poem's lack of precision about who has been killed: 'the men' (l.2) encompasses all ranks, not just the officer class with which the author of passage B is acquainted. This broad concern may be seen as appropriate for a poem of humane lament.

The prose text's particularity, on the other hand, both narrows the focus and sharpens the political implications. Thus, if we do share its sentiments (defined quite precisely and unambiguously in the phrase 'my anti-war ideas', l.17), we are likely to find its limitations acceptable. After all, the fact that the writer is a member of a privileged class does not invalidate his point of view. Moreover, he is careful to ensure that his opinions are based on measured, not rash, reflections. He avoids emotive responses by pointing out how an immediate and powerful experience inevitably provokes an irrational reaction. At the front, this takes the form of 'the emotional "happy warrior" attitude . . . so helpful in sustaining one's fortitude' (ll.19–21). At home, it is his irrational hostility to 'the graciously-organized amenities of Chapelwood Manor' (ll.14–15). The retrospective nature of the description of both environments is emphasized by the repeated use of the pluperfect tense ('had healed', 'had been followed', ll.1, 2; 'had been in abeyance', 'had been too busy', ll.17, 17–18). Both, that is, are seen as evoking strong immediate responses, but also, after a time, more tempered reflections. The writer's detachment thus provides a rational basis for the attitudes he presents. Placed above and beyond any propaganda battle, the sentiments appear both measured and convincing.

(xvi)

In this extract from a long poem, the speaker considers how different characters in ancient Greece might have responded to their environment.

'Once more to distant ages of the world
Let us revert, and place before our thoughts
The face which rural solitude might wear
To the unenlightened swains of pagan Greece.
5   — In that fair clime, the lonely herdsman, stretched
On the soft grass through half a summer's day,
With music lulled his indolent repose:
And, in some fit of weariness, if he,
When his own breath was silent, chanced to hear
10 A distant strain, far sweeter than the sounds
Which his poor skill could make, his fancy fetched,
Even from the blazing chariot of the sun,
A beardless Youth, who touched a golden lute,
And filled the illumined groves with ravishment.
15 The nightly hunter, lifting a bright eye
Up towards the crescent moon, with grateful heart
Called on the lovely wanderer who bestowed
That timely light, to share his joyous sport:
And hence, a beaming Goddess with her Nymphs,
20 Across the lawn and through the darksome grove,
Not unaccompanied with tuneful notes
By echo multiplied from rock or cave,
Swept in the storm of chase; as moon and stars
Glance rapidly along the clouded heaven,
25 When winds are blowing strong. The traveller slaked
His thirst from rill or gushing fount, and thanked
The Naiad. Sunbeams, upon distant hills
Gliding apace, with shadows in their train,
Might, with small help from fancy, be transformed
30 Into fleet Oreads sporting visibly.
The Zephyrs fanning, as they passed, their wings,
Lacked not, for love, fair objects whom they wooed
With gentle whisper. Withered boughs grotesque,
Stripped of their leaves and twigs by hoary age,
35 From depth of shaggy covert peeping forth
In the low vale, or on steep mountain-side;
And, sometimes, intermixed with stirring horns
Of the live deer, or goat's depending beard, —
These were the lurking Satyrs, a wild brood

40   Of gamesome Deities; or Pan himself,
      The simple shepherd's awe-inspiring God!'

Although the speaker begins by inviting us to consider how nature
might have appeared to the ancient Greeks, the passage actually presents his or her own highly imaginative version of their experience. The
speaker's own historical period is undetermined, but the fact that he or
she can conceive of how the Greeks felt and saw the presence of Gods,
Goddesses, and lesser deities in their 'rural solitude' (l.3) indicates the
enduring and potent presence of Greek literature and mythology in the
literature and culture of later ages.

   Ironically, the speaker limits his or her reference to 'unenlightened
swains' (l.4), yet it is only a sophisticated, educated person of a later
age – poet, speaker, or reader – who is able to imagine Apollo, say,
the 'beardless Youth' of l.13, or Artemis (the Roman Diana), the 'Goddess with her Nymphs' at l.19, even though the general allusion to
mythological characters is clear to all. The speaker's conceptions imply
that this divide was not to be found in ancient Greece, the democratic
association between Gods and humble folk culminating in the climax
of the last two lines: 'or Pan himself,/The simple shepherd's awe-
inspiring God!'' ' Where such an easy, ideal, yet breath-taking relationship is thought to exist between the very widest extremes of social
hierarchy – from 'swains' to immortals – it is appropriate that the
speaker should employ the dignity of blank verse to expound his or her
conceptions. This might be contrasted with the dramatic example (iii),
where the defects in the lord's behaviour suggest that prose, rather than
blank verse, would have been more suitable for what he had to say.
Here, however, blank verse is also more fitting as the form which has
often been seen as the closest English equivalent to the unrhymed
poetry of the Ancients themselves.

   Yet it remains a debatable point how far the speaker evokes a true
picture of life in 'pagan Greece', or how far it is simply a product of his
or her own imagination. Familiar with, and stimulated by, what we
assume to be a reading of classical texts in which appear 'Naiad[s]'
(l.27), 'Oreads' (l.30), and 'Zephyrs' (l.31), the speaker assumes an
uncomplicated relationship between literature and real life. At first, he
or she is careful to maintain a degree of speculation, 'the face which
rural solitude might wear' (l.3), and suggests it is the lonely herdsman's
'fancy' which evoked the God Apollo to explain the 'distant strain, far
sweeter than the sounds/Which his poor skill could make' (ll.10–11).
When we get to the 'nightly hunter' (l.15), however, it is as if Artemis
'with her Nymphs' actually appears in person – 'And hence, a beaming
Goddess' (l.19). Similarly, the 'traveller . . . thanked/The Naiad' for
quenching his thirst as though the water nymph was a real presence
about the 'rill or gushing fount' (ll.25–27); whereas there is a return,

almost grudgingly, to '*small* help from fancy [our emphasis]' to transform 'sunbeams' to 'fleet Oreads' (ll.27–30). Zephyrs are made synonymous with breezes; while 'withered boughs', together with 'horns/Of the live deer, or goat's depending beard, – /These were the lurking Satyrs . . . [even] Pan himself . . .' (ll.33–40), where, ironically, the speaker's fanciful excitement lends a certainty (note the emphasis on 'These') which has lost sight of fancy's part altogether. You might be reminded of Part I, section (iii), where we remarked that an enthusiastic engagement with literature can dissolve the boundaries between the real and the illusory. Although the speaker attributes the confusion here of 'fact' and fancy to 'unenlightened swains', it is he or she, of course, who is presuming to describe their attitudes. The entire passage reveals his or her responses at least as much as what theirs might have been. This bridges the gap between his or her own sophistication and their supposed simplicity, just as he or she conceives of the deities themselves in familiar association with rural people.

Writers, and the speakers they create, to some extent inevitably shape the past in their own image and that of the age to which they belong. History, of a literary or seemingly more 'factual' kind, cannot be impartial as our analysis of examples (iv) emphasizes. Here, at the most prosaic level, we could discount the whole passage on the grounds that gods and goddesses simply do not, and never did, exist. That the speaker's language wants to have it otherwise not only suggests his or her own excitement, but also the presence of a living Greek tradition, in the context of which the reader might appreciate this passage. A vital, complementary tradition is also alluded to in the speaker's reflection upon the 'lonely herdsman, stretched/On the soft grass through half a summer's day' (ll.5–6). This idealization of rural life, rather than engagement with the day-to-day labours of the shepherd, calls to mind the literary convention known as Pastoral. It is a form of great antiquity (Theocritus, the major Greek exponent, lived in the fourth and third centuries BC), extending in various guises into at least the nineteenth century (Shelley's *Adonais*, for example). The allusion to this literary tradition in a passage supposedly calling to mind the real life of rural Greece only reinforces our sense of the complex interrelationship between literature and life.

The problems involved in a retrospective account are conveniently located in the speaker's collective description of the characters as 'unenlightened swains of pagan Greece'. These 'swains' never saw themselves as 'pagan' – on the contrary, with such apparent belief in, and closeness to, their divinities nothing could have been further from their thoughts. They can only be seen to be so from the vantage point of some later Christian period. Similarly, the description of them as 'unenlightened' not only conceives of them as simple, unlettered or uneducated, but also 'unenlightened' in the sense of lacking the knowledge of later Christian revelation, from which perspective the one true God banished all others. Yet we have noted the speaker's keenness to evoke a landscape peopled with 'pagan' deities and how this ironically suggests an identification with those depicted as simple people. The passage, then, reveals no derision of these 'swains', which would make the irony something other than of a gentle kind. Rather, in imagining how these rural characters are moved to gracious thoughts through having their environment populated with deities, it is suggested that something virtuous and beautiful has since been lost. The 'distant strain' is made that much more ravishing by the lonely weary herdsman's imaginative wish to attribute it to Apollo, which eradicates any sense of jealousy he might otherwise have felt when, 'silent', he heard music 'far sweeter' than his own. The nightly hunter who 'with grateful heart/Called on the lovely warrior . . . to share his joyous sport' (ll.16–18), and the traveller who 'thanked/The Naiad' for the assuaging of his thirst are both morally and imaginatively enhanced by being seen to respond so directly to this mythological world. That sunbeams might be transformed into 'fleet Oreads' (l.30), or 'withered boughs grotesque' (l.33) take part in the change to 'lurking Satyrs, a wild brood/Of gamesome Deities; or Pan himself' (ll.39–40) suggests an imaginative resource available to all ancient Greeks which complements the promptings to moral gratitude (these possibilities are not necessarily restricted to the traveller of l.25). That the ideal has been made real reveals the speaker's own desires for a fully integrated life of goodness and imagination, for a 'golden age', and illustrates in a representative way why it is that successive epochs have been inspired by their responses to the world of antiquity.

(xvii)

In the following letter, the Victorian novelist Thackeray congratulates Frederick Gale on his forthcoming marriage.

Kensington. August 23.

My dear Gale.

I send your boots and my blessing. I am very glad to hear of what is going to happen to you and heartily wish health and happiness to a good fellow and his wife.

5   Always treat her as if she was the finest lady in England. Never be rude to your wife: that's the advice I give you. Not that I fancy you will: but many men are, and ruin their homes by it. Did you ever see my step-father & mother? I think not. Well, he is 70 odd & she 60. He pays
10 her to this day as much deference, as he did when he first stepped up to her at a Bath Ball in 1807, and asked her to dance. She was one of the most beautiful women in the world — I am considered very like her. Those 2 folks are to this day, though old, disappointed, and with many cares & crosses in life, immensely happy in each others affection; and it's because they have always respected each other.

15   I could shew you quite a different story and a ménage that promised every happiness, (where the man was a good fellow, & the woman a mere angel,) rendered miserable by the man forgetting he was a gentleman, and a lady's husband. So I say unto you, my dear old Gale, Be polite to your wife, as you are now at this present time of courtship.

20   Where's the marriage to be? I am nailed pretty much here now having business and 100 reasons but I should like to see you set out on your journey & with all my heart wish it may be a happy one.

Yours dear Gale most truly

W M Thackeray

I am only just back from 6 weeks abroad, with my children.

To read a letter of this kind may seem to be an intrusion upon a private relationship. The publication of letters written by famous people is, however, a reflection of a general wish to know as much as possible about them. As we say in Part I (iii), anything authors have written is likely to be of interest to the biographical critic. If confronted with a letter for literary analysis, we face a particular problem: we shall probably know nothing of the relationship between the writer and the recipient of the letter, and therefore be ignorant of the circumstances out of which it has been written.

In the present case, we cannot be expected to know how friendly

Thackeray and Gale were, or at what stage in the novelist's career this letter was composed. Inferences can, however, be drawn, if treated with care. We can note the friendly and yet not entirely informal address ('My dear Gale', not 'Dear Sir' or even 'Dear Gale', but not 'Dear Frederick'), and the similar tone of the signing-off ('Yours . . . truly', not 'Yours faithfully', balanced by the warmer 'dear Gale'). But even here we must be on our guard against judging by modern, more relaxed, standards: for us to call someone by their surname seems much more formal than it would have done for a Victorian. Thackeray's relationship with Gale is certainly close enough for the sending of 'blessing' (l.2) rather than simply 'congratulations', and for him to express the wish to attend the wedding.

The quality of the relationship between writer and addressee will, of course, determine the tone adopted. Yet the peculiarity of this letter is the extent to which it combines friendly banter with serious admonition. It looks as if Thackeray is both an equal and an older man, speaking out of assumed superiority.

This variation in tone is most marked in the sudden change from the first to the second paragraph. Thackeray begins by jokily combining boots with blessing, an instance of comic alliteration in which the words so associated are of a very different kind (here one is abstract and serious, the other comically material). He then straightforwardly declares his pleasure at the news of Gale's intended marriage, employing the common alliterative wish, 'health and happiness', and adding an appropriate touch of heartiness by calling him a 'good fellow' (ll.3–4).

But the second paragraph opens with direct commands: 'Always treat her . . . Never be rude . . .' (ll.5–6). This 'advice' (l.6) is supported by open moralizing on the disastrous results of men's failure to act by it. Thackeray is himself polite enough, or politic enough, to make it clear that he thinks that Gale will not treat his wife improperly ('Not that I fancy you will', l.6); but the warning is still given in extreme terms ('ruin their homes', l.7). Like all good moralizers, Thackeray illustrates his lesson with a positive example. Gale himself is presumed to be behaving towards his future wife with the 'deference' (l.9) shown by Thackeray's step-father at the Bath Ball; the lesson, then, is to continue to show the same regard through all the difficulties which their life together may bring ('cares & crosses', l.13) so that they, too, will preserve 'affection' (l.13) sustained by mutual respect.

We might note here the level of the social world implied by the story: in early-nineteenth-century England (the date, 1807, specifies the time as just before the period known as the Regency), Bath was one of the major meeting-places for fashionable society. You may know of Jane Austen's depiction of Bath society at that time in *Northanger Abbey*. A Bath Ball would therefore be a high-point of the season, a fitting moment for the display of socially attractive manners. Such deferential male treatment of women reflects suggestively on the social and moral attitudes which lie behind the letter. The quality Thackeray singles out in the step-father is his 'deference', in his mother it is her beauty (l.11). In the third paragraph, the alternative story of an unnamed couple – the warning to set alongside the good example of Thackeray's parents – has as its moral that happiness can only be preserved if a man does not forget to be a 'gentleman, and a lady's husband' (ll.17–18). The warning is precisely aimed at Gale by the repetition from the first paragraph of the phrase 'good fellow' (l.16). The unnamed man, too, was once what Gale is now; and he admired his wife in the way that Gale, presumably, does his fiancée (a 'mere angel', l.17). Some words shift in meaning over time, and 'mere' could mean 'perfect', 'to the fullest extent', as well as 'barely', the modern sense. In this context we are likely to assume that Thackeray has the former in mind. This idealization of the woman is reflected in the social deference recommended by Thackeray. The moral seems to be that, although all men idealize their wives at the beginning of a marriage, true happiness can only be secured by sustaining that idealization in their life together. This is what it is to be a real 'gentleman'. We might consider whether for a modern reader a more honest appreciation of each partner's vices and virtues would be a better recipe for success.

Moralizing though the tone of all this may be, Thackeray is careful to moderate it by returning to the more friendly address of the opening. He may, indeed, have prepared the ground for this in the middle of his advice. When he describes his mother as having been 'one of the most beautiful women in the world' (ll.10–11), he adds the irrelevant 'I am considered very like her' (l.11). At first sight, this may appear to be simply vanity; but it may be the case that Thackeray is inserting some mock-vanity, or even irony, which he knows Gale will recognize and smile at. However one interprets this, it is clear that the final statement of the moral (ll.18–19) is introduced by a return to familiarity ('my dear old Gale'), and by the self-consciously pompous 'So I say unto you', where the mock-biblical phraseology nicely undercuts the parable form (where story exemplifies moral) which the writer has been adopting for his message.

This return to familiarity enables the entire final paragraph to be pitched at the same frank and friendly level as the opening, with terms from the first paragraph being repeated: 'heartily' (l.3)/'all my heart' (l.22), 'happiness' (l.3)/'happy' (l.22). The use of colloquial language ('I am nailed pretty much . . .', l.20) contributes to the establishment of a tone of friendly chat. The postscript, too, can be seen as providing a human touch, as Thackeray sends Gale news about himself. But there are also implications which reflect on the more serious parts of the letter. First, the mention of his children shows that the writer is an established family man (and, presumably, older than Gale), so allowing him to speak with the authority of experience. And yet there is no mention of a wife. This is a case where a knowledge of the writer's life would certainly suggest why he might be placing such solemn importance on a happy marriage; for Thackeray's own much-loved wife fell a victim to mental illness at an early stage of their marriage. Whatever the validity or invalidity of speculation on the basis of this knowledge, it should be clear from the letter itself that the advice about happiness in marriage is founded on an awareness of the problems of life. Thackeray sees marriage as a journey (l.22), the possible misfortunes of which are exemplified by the 'cares & crosses' endured by the happy couple. We might note that Thackeray's mother's journey has been eventful: the references in the second paragraph are to his stepfather. Her first husband had died in his thirties, and only then did she become the wife of the man she had met at the Bath Ball while still a single woman.

(xviii)

These two passages present contrasting accounts of school-teaching. The first is from a verse-epistle (a letter in verse), the second from a novel.

A.   The only thing you never turned your hand to
       Was teaching English in a boarding school.
    Today it's a profession that seems grand to
       Those whose alternative's an office stool;
5   For budding authors it's become the rule.
    To many an unknown genius postmen bring
    Typed notices from Rabbitarse and String.

    The Head's M.A., a bishop is a patron,
       The assistant staff is highly qualified;
10   Health is the care of an experienced matron,
       The arts are taught by ladies from outside;
       The food is wholesome and the grounds are wide;
    The aim is training character and poise,
    With special coaching for the backward boys.

15   I found the pay good and had time to spend it,
       Though others may not have the good luck I did:
    For you I'd hesitate to recommend it;
       Several have told me that they can't abide it,
       Still, if one tends to get a bit one-sided,
20   It's pleasant as it's easy to secure
    The hero worship of the immature.

B.   Mr Osmand taught French and very occasionally Latin at the modest unambitious filthy little school which I attended. He had been at the school for many years but I did not become his pupil until I was about fourteen, with my loutish reputation well developed. I had, until then,
5 learnt practically nothing. I could (just) read, but although I had attended classes in history and French and mathematics I had imbibed extremely little of these subjects. The realization that people had simply given up trying to teach me anything enlightened me at last, more than the lectures from magistrates, about how utterly ship-wrecked I was; and
10 increased my anger and my sense of injustice. For with the dawning despair came also the tormenting idea that in spite of everything I was clever, I had a mind though I had never wanted to use it. I *could* learn things, only now it was too late and nobody would let me. Mr Osmand looked at me quietly. He had grey eyes. He gave me his full *attention*.
15   I suspect that many children are saved by saints and geniuses of this kind. Why are such people not made rich by a grateful society? How

exactly the miracle happened is another thing which I cannot very clearly recall. Suddenly my mind woke up. Floods of light came in. I began to learn. I began to want to excel in new ways. I learnt French. I started on
20   Latin. Mr Osmand promised me Greek. An ability to write fluent correct Latin prose began to offer me an escape from (perhaps literally) the prison house, began in time to show me vistas headier and more glorious than any I had ever before known how to dream of.

As is often the case in comparison and contrast exercises, similarity of subject-matter is here less important than differences in style, form and point of view. It would be difficult, indeed, to find two more dissimilar passages in terms of their attitudes to teaching and schoolteachers.

The prose text approaches the subject from the serious perspective of a late-developing student, who discovers his ability to learn through the influence of an individual teacher. The first paragraph begins and ends with the teacher, Mr Osmand, introducing him in merely factual terms (the subjects he taught, how long he had been at the school), and concluding with three short sentences (ll.13–14) which appear at first sight to be similarly straightforward. But the clue to the underlying meaning lies in the word which is italicized for emphasis, *'attention'*: the narrator's perception of his grey eyes tells us that Osmand's quiet look has been returned, that communication has been established. This relationship is between two individuals. Mr Osmand (his name, the mark of his identity, begins the passage) is the only teacher named, a reflection of his unique status in the narrator's view of the school. The others are collected in the vaguest possible way as 'people' (l.7) who gave up trying to teach someone whose 'loutish reputation' (l.4) – the word 'loutish' indicates that the speaker is male – presumably formed their attitude towards him. If the phrase evokes general prejudices, then it leads to prejudgement of the individual concerned. Similarly ineffectual were the 'lectures' (ll.8–9) of unnamed magistrates. Lectures, the implication seems to be, are delivered impersonally, whereas genuine teaching engages two individuals in direct contact.

Everything in the text serves to heighten the contrast between the student's experiences before and after meeting Mr Osmand. The school itself is scathingly described as 'modest unambitious filthy little', the four derogatory adjectives run into one another without punctuation as a reflection of the narrator's total dismissal of its dowdy unprogressiveness. His lack of educational attainment, quite spectacular for someone who has reached the age of fourteen, is countered by the impressive speed of his learning under Osmand (pace being created by the novelist's use of short sentences, ll.18–20). His generous tribute to such teachers is couched in the dramatically extreme terms of saving a pupil from the ship-wreck (l.9) of his present life and the literal and metaphorical prison (l.22) which beckons in the future. Use of religious vocabulary ('saved by saints', l.15; 'miracle', l.17) adds to the sense of a dramatic conversion, a seeing of the light (cf. 'Floods of light came in', l.18).

By contrast, the poem is written from the point of view of a teacher, and one at a very different kind of school. The second stanza establishes precisely the social and educational pretensions of a boarding-school, describing it in general terms as characteristic of its kind, rather than as a specific example. Each element of the description is carefully judged for its satirical purpose: rather than make direct critical comments, the poet lists apparently innocuous statements whose effectiveness lies in their implications. The academic and social tone is set by the Head's MA. (probably an Oxford or Cambridge first degree); the Church of England provides socially respectable, but not too elevated (a bishop, not an archbishop), patronage; and the dominant male atmosphere of the school is suggested by the conventional limitation of female roles to health and the arts ('matron', l.10, is a safe authority figure, while the more dangerous arts are allocated to 'ladies' – not 'women' – 'from outside', l.11). The extensiveness of the grounds neatly suggests both wealth in possession of property and a stereotyped public-school enthusiasm for sports to set against the implied attitude to the arts. The couplet at the end of the stanza sums up the aims of the school as 'training character and poise' (l.13) – personal and social qualities rather than intellectual abilities – while unspecified 'special coaching' (the noun itself is more suited to games than academic subjects) awaits 'backward boys' (l.14). This group would, presumably, include the narrator of passage B, were he to be in such a school. Attitudes are thus starkly contrasted: the pupil who receives special treatment at one school would be abandoned in the other.

The language of the texts is equally contrasted. Whereas passage B preserves a seriousness of tone to reflect the narrator's commitment to his achievements (as in the use of religious language for personal experience, set against the institutionalized religion of the poem), the poet adopts a consistently comic tone to create a wry, sceptical attitude. The humour is at its broadest in the invented name 'Rabbitarse and String' (l.7), where, although the specific reference will not be clear without a knowledge of the context of the passage (the phrase actually parodies the name of a teaching agency), the vulgarity is obviously mocking in attitude. More generally, the comic tone is furnished by the humorous rhymes, in particular feminine rhymes (rhymes of two syllables, the second of which is unstressed) which are ingenious ('hand to'/'grand to', ll.1 and 3) or which link significant details ('patron'/'matron', ll.8 and 10, contrasting male and female roles). The stanza-form is an abbreviated version of the *ottava rima* (a b a b a b c c) employed notably for comic effects by Byron. As with *ottava rima*, the stanza-form allows the poet to build up to a climactic or anti-climactic couplet. 'Rabbitarse and String' is the most obvious example of the rhyming couplet being used to deflate, in this case the pretensions of a self-styled 'unknown genius' (l.6). Rhymes throughout can be used for such effects, as when the 'boarding school'/'office stool' (ll.2 and 4) rhyme degrades the profession of the teacher and his place of work by making it just a means of escaping from the unglamorous life of an office clerk.

This comic tone is appropriate for the poet's disparaging account of a teacher's life: indeed, the tone actually helps to create that account. Teaching is something which one turns one's hand to (l.1), as if a hobby or an odd job rather than a calling; and something which is chosen for negative reasons (ll.3–4). Its principal merits are the distinctly pragmatic ones of providing good pay and the time to spend it (l.15), and even then the poet would not generally recommend it (ll.17–18). This teacher's-eye view of teaching is thus the opposite of the pupil's view of the Osmands of the profession, who are elevated into saviour-figures.

The connection between the two otherwise directly contrasting texts lies in each writer's capacity to use language creatively. An English teacher who is or was a 'budding author' (l.5) demonstrates his ability to manipulate an elaborate stanza-form; while Mr Osmand opens up for the narrator of passage B vistas of languages, ancient and modern. His ability to learn languages then becomes an ability to use them himself ('to write fluent correct Latin prose', ll.20–21). A positive view of the power of languages lies behind the seriousness of the autobiographical account. That the student has developed into the author of the text we are reading indicates how knowledge of the forms of foreign languages has been complemented by a capacity to employ those of his native tongue. It may be, then, that the poet's facility with language reflects his off-hand view of teaching, while the narrator's testimony to the power of teaching bespeaks his struggle to acquire knowledge. Significantly, the concluding couplet of passage A, with its confession of a selfish and potentially sinister manipulation of a teacher's role, provides a cynical alternative to the ideal described in passage B: where a teacher sees how tempting and easy it may be to engineer ('secure', l.20) hero worship, a student genuinely attests to the existence of heroes.

(xix)

This is an excerpt from a critical essay on the novels of the Brontë sisters.

> The meaning of a book, which lies so often apart from what happens and
> what is said and consists rather in some connection which things in
> themselves different have had for the writer, is necessarily hard to
> grasp. Especially this is so when, like the Brontës, the writer is poetic
> 5   and his meaning inseparable from his language, and itself rather a mood
> than a particular observation. *Wuthering Heights* is a more difficult book
> to understand than *Jane Eyre*, because Emily was a greater poet than
> Charlotte. When Charlotte wrote, she said with eloquence and splen-
> dour and passion 'I love', 'I hate', 'I suffer'. Her experience, though more
> 10 intense, is on a level with our own. But there is no 'I' in *Wuthering
> Heights*. There are no governesses. There are no employers. There is
> love, but it is not the love of men and women. Emily was inspired by
> some more general conception. The impulse which urged her to create
> was not her own suffering or her own injuries. She looked out upon a
> 15 world cleft into gigantic disorder and felt within her the power to unite it in
> a book. That gigantic ambition is to be felt throughout the novel – a
> struggle, half thwarted but of superb conviction, to say something
> through the mouths of her characters which is not merely 'I love' or '
> hate', but 'we, the whole human race' and 'you, the eternal powers . . .
> 20 The sentence remains unfinished. It is not strange that it should be so;
> rather it is astonishing that she can make us feel what she had it in her to
> say at all. It surges up in the half-articulate words of Catherine Earnshaw
> 'If all else perished and *he* remained, I should still continue to be; and if all
> else remained and he were annihilated, the universe would turn to a
> 25 mighty stranger; I should not seem part of it'. It breaks out again in the
> presence of the dead. 'I see a repose that neither earth nor hell can
> break, and I feel an assurance of the endless and shadowless hereafter –
> the eternity they have entered – where life is boundless in its duration,
> and love in its sympathy and joy in its fulness'. It is this suggestion of
> 30 power underlying the apparitions of human nature and lifting them up into
> the presence of greatness that gives the book its huge stature among
> other novels.

To criticize the writing of a critic may seem a reductive exercise. If the
function of criticism is to help us to draw nearer to an understanding of
a text, we seem here to be stepping backwards. We are now dissecting
the dissector.

However, an exercise of this kind is actually highly appropriate for a
consideration of the value of many of the recent theoretical approaches
which we discussed in Part I. The general view that all writing, not just

that found in the conventional literary forms of poem, play and novel, is literature has gained such currency that examination boards are increasingly including a wide range of material in their criticism papers. There is no reason why literary criticism itself should be an exception.

More specifically, though, much modern theory has argued that language of all kinds creates a series of 'texts', whether written or spoken, which constitute the only 'reality' available to us. Advocates of these ideas see language as a self-referring structure; so that, for example, a novel which purports to describe a world outside itself, a life of social reality, only sets up its own internal world of language. If a novel thus forms its own world, a critical analysis of it will be similarly detached from that world which it claims to describe. Like the lover on Keats's Grecian Urn, we never win the goal. The problem of criticism is the problem of all writing.

If we adopt the terms of ideological criticism rather than those of deconstructive criticism, we can propose a more solid aim for the present exercise. The way in which we talk about a text will be determined by aspects of our own conscious or unconscious attitudes, whether to politics, religion, class, gender or whatever. Thus a piece of criticism will tell us as much about its author as about the work under discussion. We can consequently analyse a critical text in the same way that we can examine the ways in which a novel by Dickens reveals social attitudes, or a poem by Donne reflects religious or erotic feelings.

Our example raises such fundamental questions in its very first sentence. Meaning lies not in 'what happens and what is said' but in the private and separate experience of the author. But how do we recognize any meaning which does not lie in 'what happens and what is said'? If we argue that meaning can only exist in what is realized in a text, then we shall want to alter our critic's 'hard to grasp' to 'impossible to grasp'. The same principle would, therefore, apply to our reading of this passage: what 'connection which things in themselves different have had for the writer' we simply do not know.

However, that the critic does seem to believe in the possibility of recovering a meaning of this kind reveals much about his or her presuppositions. The critic tends to use terms in an imprecise manner, depending more on their rhetorical or token value than on their exact sense. 'Poetic' (l.4) is a case in point: it is used to imply a heightened imaginative power of a kind difficult to pin down ('rather a mood than a particular observation', ll.5–6). The language which is then used about Emily Brontë's *Wuthering Heights* has the same impressive vagueness. The critic's unproven assumption is that a great writer is someone who is naturally endowed with superior insight and sensibility, rather than someone whose creativity is the product of much hard labour. Emily was 'inspired by some more general conception' (ll.12–13), an 'impulse which urged her to create' (l.13). This language we would call 'Romantic', private inspiration being taken as the key value; and the terms in which the critic speaks of the novelist's vision ('a world cleft into gigantic disorder', ll.14–15) are similarly pitched at a grand level. *Wuthering Heights* speaks not of a single character or set of characters, but of the ' "whole human race" ' and ' "the eternal powers" ' (l.19). The language of the critic's definition of the novelist's aim is, paradoxically, indefinite, relying on abstract nouns ('disorder', 'powers') and adjectives which give a vague sense of exceptional value ('superb', l.17). One such adjective, 'gigantic' (ll.15–16), is significantly repeated in successive sentences so that the extreme state of the world is equated with the extreme nature of Emily Brontë's ambition.

A further device used to elevate the position of *Wuthering Heights* is that of contrast. Charlotte Brontë's *Jane Eyre* is made a foil whereby the personalized statements of the form ' "I love" ' (l.9) can be translated into the higher vision which transcends the mere love of men and women. *Jane Eyre* is thus simply a means of providing a point of distinction, which is then put aside as the passage develops into sole concentration on *Wuthering Heights*. But is the contrast a valid one? When we look at a piece of criticism, we can, of course, only begin to test its validity if we know the books under discussion. However sceptical we might be about the objective status of a text, it is difficult to deny that it possesses some certain elements of style or presentation which are open to analysis. One of these elements in *Wuthering Heights* is that the whole novel is narrated by Lockwood, even when he is mediating what other characters have told him. For all that we might lose sight of the fact – and many critics have done so – Nelly Dean's story is told to us by Lockwood and Lockwood alone. It is thus as much a first-person narrative as is *Jane Eyre*. Our critic's refusal to see, or to acknowledge, this indicates that a desire to contrast personal narration with general vision is more important to him or her than attention to essential technical details.

The critic is thus yielding to his or her vision of the novel. Fittingly then, the later part of the passage attests to the power of the work by quoting the novel's own language, extracted from the narrative context (ll.23–25, 26–29). The critic's language gives way to that of the supreme work of art, whose 'huge stature' (l.31) reflects the 'gigantic' nature of its author's vision and ambition. The chosen quotations, not surprisingly, use language similar in kind to that earlier used by the critic. We are presented with large terms ('universe', 'earth', 'hell' ll.24, 26), abstract nouns ('life', 'love', ll.28, 29) and adjectives which attribute large value ('mighty', 'endless', 'boundless', ll.25, 27, 28) Not only is the novel's language reflected in the critic's own, but the vagueness of the novel's statements is acknowledged ('half-articulate words', l.22) and, indeed, seen as essential to the grandeur of its subject-matter. When we are dealing with vast themes, sentences have to remain incompleted (l.20), as language cannot fully encompass the ideas (cf. passage (vi)). Only by reproducing the effects of the novel, either by use of similar language or by direct quotation, can the critic's language find an appropriate form. Thus the work of criticism partakes of the qualities – good or bad – which it perceives in the work criticized.

Does all criticism, then, simply re-enact its subject? Or is our example unacceptably impressionistic, a proof of the need for greater scientific rigour in our analyses? What would I. A. Richards have thought of it?

(xx)

The following is an extract from a long poem in which the speaker celebrates his identity.

> I am the poet of the Body and I am the poet of the Soul,
> The pleasures of heaven are with me and the pains of hell are with me,
> The first I graft and increase upon myself, the latter I translate into a new tongue.
>
> I am the poet of the woman the same as the man,
> 5 And I say it is as great to be a woman as to be a man,
> And I say there is nothing greater than the mother of men.
>
> I chant the chant of dilation or pride,
> We have had ducking and deprecating about enough,
> I show that size is only development.
>
> 10 Have you outstript the rest? are you the President?
> It is a trifle, they will more than arrive there every one, and still pass on.
> I am he that walks with the tender and growing night,
> I call to the earth and sea half-held by the night.
>
> Press close bare-bosom'd night — press close magnetic nourishing night!
> 15 Night of south winds — night of the large few stars
> Still nodding night — mad naked summer night.
>
> Smile O voluptuous cool-breath'd earth!
> Earth of the slumbering and liquid trees!
> Earth of departed sunset — earth of the mountains misty-topt!
> 20 Earth of the vitreous pour of the full moon just tinged with blue!
> Earth of shine and dark mottling the tide of the river!
> Earth of the limpid grey of clouds brighter and clearer for my sake!
> Far-swooping elbow'd earth — rich apple-blossom'd earth!
> Smile, for your lover comes.
> 25 Prodigal, you have given me love — therefore I to you give love!
> O unspeakable passionate love.

The most immediately striking quality of this extract is the grammatical dominance of the first-person singular pronoun. Each of the first three units of verse begins with 'I'. Each of these units consists of a complete sentence, so that the first three sentences all begin with 'I'. Within each sentence verbs are repeated and varied in order to allow further emphasis on the recurring first-person subject. Later variation of syntax still returns to the simple 'I' + verb pattern, the rhetorical questions of line 10 being followed by a repetition of the opening 'I am' at line 12, and the exclamatory addresses to the earth giving way eventually to 'I to you give love' at line 25. The entire passage is, that is to say, frankly, even brazenly, egotistic – egotism being defined as frequent or excessive use of the first-person singular pronoun.

We are, then, far away from that ideal of objectivity gained by subordination of the artist's personality, which such writers as T.S. Eliot have advocated. Here the poet's personality imposes itself upon the subject-matter. Subjectivity is flaunted in a manner which recalls a central text of the so-called 'Romantic' movement, Jean-Jacques Rousseau's *Confessions*, which begins by announcing that the author wishes to reveal to the reader a man in all the truth of nature – 'et cet homme ce sera moi' ('and this man will be me'). In our own century there has even emerged a school of poetry which have been given the name 'confessional'.

The writer here seeks to define his identity in terms of a poetic voice. The repeated 'I am the poet' of the opening lines of the first two units of verse makes the claim starkly, while other verbs continue the idea of a speaking voice – 'I say', ll.5–6; 'I call', l.13 – and develop it specifically into linguistic and poetic directions – 'I translate', l.3; 'I chant', l.7. The notion of song here echoes a fundamental conception of the poet as singer, which has informed poetic theory and practice through the ages, perhaps most significantly and memorably in the formulaic opening of classical epic, as in Virgil's 'arma virumque cano' ('arms and the man I sing'). The word 'chant', indeed, derives ultimately from the Latin verb 'canere' ('to sing'). The poet's identity, then, is ostentatiously identified with the rôle of inspired and ambitious singer.

His aspirations are pitched at an equivalently high level. The opening line of the first unit combines body and soul, while that of the second unit combines female and male. The first, that is, unites the totality of our common conception of a human being, while the second unites the whole human race. This claim of all-inclusiveness both matches and qualifies the egotism: it reflects the huge nature of the ambition (or, if one chooses to be critical, of the conceit), but it also rejects the idea of egotism as separation of the self from the world in favour of an embracing of the world. We might consider here a possible self-contradiction within the stance adopted, for it is arguable that an assertion of all-inclusiveness actually reduces the rest of the world to the measure of the poet's own personality, rather than subsuming that personality into the consciousness of the rest of humanity. You might recall our observation in Part I section (iii) about how some feminist theories see male attempts to acknowledge female experience as a form of appropriation, since their discourse remains inevitably male-orientated. A similar objection might, then, be lodged against the attitudes adopted in this text.

Such doubts do not trouble the poet, however. The challenging, even shocking, confidence of his assertions continues in the third unit of verse as, with heavy and insistent alliteration, he rejects humility ('ducking and deprecating') in favour of pride, thus converting into a virtue what is traditionally regarded as a vice. The exact nature of the ideal he advocates remains undefined, although its magnitude is conveyed by the way in which size is seen approvingly as an indication of development (l.9).

The remainder of the extract seeks to suggest its nature, first by a negative, (ll.10–11) then by an expansive positive (ll.12–26). It is not to be defined as fame of the kind which the world acknowledges: the status of President, the supreme political power in the land (the title suggests that the provenance of the text is America, or, at any rate, not Britain), is dismissed as a 'trifle' (ll.10–11) which will be surpassed in the people's development. The passage then focuses upon the natural world as the sphere of the poet's sel-realization and, presumably, that of 'every one' (l.11). He embraces – the word is appropriate for the expression of love in the last two lines – a breadth of natural phenomena: night with its stars and moon, the elements of water in sea and river, air in winds and sky, and, particularly, the earth of trees and blossom. The natural world is viewed in inclusive variety, pursuing the notion of comprehensiveness which has been marked in the passage throughout. This world, indeed, itself merges into a totality, as when trees (earth) are described as 'liquid' (l.18), one element being interfused with another. The relationship between poet and nature is a physically intense one (note, for example, the repetition of 'press' in line 14 and the 'passionate' of the last line), and one of mutual love. The earth is itself physically intense ('voluptuous', l.17), and it gives its love as freely to the poet as he returns it (l.25).

The eroticism of the relationship, mirroring the first line's announcement of the writer as 'poet of the Body', is linguistically conveyed by the rhapsodic tone. This is created by the succession of one-line exclamations from line 17 to line 23, the extravagantly descriptive language (e.g. 'the vitreous pour of the full moon', l.20), and such rhetorical devices as verbal repetition, a prominent feature of the passage throughout, but particularly forceful in lines 18 to 22 where each line begins with the same phrase, a resounding 'Earth of' (a device known technically as anaphora).

It is by such linguistic patternings that the poet organizes the flexible free verse. The opening line, for example, balances repetition ('I am the poet of the . . .') and antithesis (Body/Soul) in its two halves; the long unit of verse from line 17 to line 24 frames its ecstatic exclamations by a repetition of 'Smile'; and anaphora operates on a smaller scale at lines 5 and 6, giving deliberate emphasis to the poet's sententious pronouncements. Free verse could be regarded as the appropriate medium for this kind of subject-matter: a tone of enthusiastic rapture demands freedom and space. The real question, though, about the passage's effectiveness – leaving aside our attitude to the egotism and the large claims he makes – must relate to the insistent, obtrusive rhetoric. The poet declares in the last line that the love he gives and receives is 'unspeakable' – i.e. incapable of being expressed. Is this simply another rhetorical device, an attempt to make large claims by defining as indescribable that which the poem has been forcefully describing; or does it betray a sense of doubt and inadequacy? The reader has then to consider whether the language used reflects any real experience or exists merely as rhetorical bluster.

(xxi)

This passage describes the experiences of two medical students in a class on dissection.

I was on the head and neck. Birrell was on the arm. He was digging into the antecubital fossa in front of the elbow. I was telling him about the glories and importance of the lingual nerve. The professor blew along suddenly and interrupted us.

5   'If there were less talk there would be more concentration. It is better to dissect in silence. There is nothing more distracting than talk. You, Ouseley, should try to expose the lingual nerve without cutting Wharton's duct. Be careful just there. Use the handle of the knife.'

'That nerve is mightier than the sword,' Birrell ventured.

10   'What do you mean?'

It was my turn. I didn't want to let Birrell in for all the irreverence.

'I was just telling Birrell when you came along, sir, that the lingual can move masses and can make wars and found cities.'

'By wagging the tongue it wags the world, so Ouseley says.'

15   The professor grew silent so suddenly that it amounted to a gasp.

'Do you believe that, Birrell?'

'Well, sir, allowing for Ouseley's poetic imagination.'

'The lingual nerve is *entirely* sensory,' said the professor with emphasis, as he somewhat abruptly went away.

20   'Now we're boiled,' said Birrell sadly.

'Yes,' I agreed. 'It was a bad break. I'm sorry for letting you in for it. What nerve does move the tongue, anyway? One would think from its name that it was the lingual.'

'Names in anatomy are put in to mislead us,' Birrell thought. 'Let us ask

25   Williams when he comes in for the foot.'

Instead of lifting man above the beasts as I thought, the lingual nerve has filled him up with wine, spirits and beer for consumption on the premises, so to speak, and brought him down at times. Store Street and Vine Street can witness to its being 'entirely sensory'. A nerve of taste

30   indeed!

The narrator, Ouseley, a participant in the experience he relates, at once introduces us to the contrasts which enliven the entire passage: the scientific, matter of fact approach to the discipline of dissection and anatomy set against, and relieved by, the fanciful, even facetious, attitude summed up in his companion Birrell's ' "Well, sir, allowing for Ouseley's poetic imagination" ' (l.17). The reader is surprised, not to say shocked, by the deadpan manner of the first two lines, where the process of 'digging' into the corpse is only partially alleviated by the precise anatomical term which follows. Although the dissecting laboratory is not the place for sentiment, the two students appear to sense the need themselves for some kind of relief, the 'glories and importance of the lingual nerve' (l.3) emerging, as we see later, as an extempore piece of witty extravagance. The colloquial description of the professor's arrival on the scene ('blew along' l.3) itself indicates how their seemingly casual mood renders them vulnerable to his sober criticism of their conversation. 'There is nothing more distracting than talk' (l.6) draws attention to the contrast between the need for silent investigation in this branch of medical science and the urge on the part of the young men to embroider their activities.

The narrator is fully appreciative of their 'irreverence' (l.11) – irreverence, it seems, towards both the professor and the practice they are engaged upon. Ultimately it is the irreverence, or apparent irresponsibility, of the 'poetical' in the face of the scientific – the age-old conflict between the two cultures, stretching back as far as Plato, who distrusted the presence of the poet figure in his serious-minded, pragmatic commonwealth. The task here is an unpleasant even if a necessary one; yet is it not the case that the professorial approach and the students', ironically, are the same: each, in its own way, seeking to make the cutting up of bodies as manageable as possible? In hospitals, it is the surgeons who relieve the harrowing nature of their profession by their characteristically immaculate dress and choice of vocabulary when in their consulting rooms with patients. Here, however, the professor is by nature and training utterly incapable of warming to the poetical licence of his students, endeavouring only to correct their factual error over the lingual nerve, which emphatically terminates their exchange at lines 18–19. What the reader appreciates is that there is room for flexibility, the salve of the comic touch which, rather than interrupting anatomical efficiency, actually helps its practitioners to carry it out. It also has the benefit of fostering a *camaraderie*, where both Birrell and Ouseley are eager to support each other throughout the professorial scrutiny.

Left to themselves, they regain the intimacies of colloquial language ('Now we're boiled' l.20) following the self-conscious address to 'sir', the professor, previously. It is surely rough justice when, in learing that the 'lingual nerve' is *not* what its name suggests (ll.22–23), they find themselves chastised for fanciful talking inspired by readily understandable factual error. This prompts Birrell's ' "Names in anatomy are put in to mislead us" ' (l.24). Science, medical science, it seems, is just as 'distracting' (see l.6), just as misleading in its own way as the poetical flights of fancy which got them into trouble in the first place. Indeed, it is the very 'fact' of the misleading name for the nerve, enshrined, presumably, in anatomical dictionaries, which stimulated the narrator's 'glories and importance' (l.3) from the start. 'By wagging the tongue it wags the world', Birrell reports Ouseley as saying. What we discover is that medical science, in seeking to stabilize the referential nature of language, stabilize definitions, has wagged the tongues of its two less than sober minded students. It is language itself, perhaps, which 'wags the world', rather than vice-versa. 'Poetic imagination' and science, in this instance at least, prove ironically to be bedfellows, and medical science has been hoist with its own petard. With clever comic deflation, it regains a less than subtle grounding with Birrell's ' "Let us ask Williams when he comes in for the foot" ' (ll.24-25). Lingual nerves might not be what you think lingual nerves ought to be, but at least a foot is a foot.

Disappointed but not entirely dispirited, Ouseley still rescues what he can for the 'poetic imagination' in his final reflective paragraph. But the scientific definition of the lingual nerve as '*entirely* sensory' (l.18) has, in effect, deprived the 'world' of that eloquence which, paradoxically, he still wittily pursues in imaging how said nerve has merely served to excite our appetites for alcohol. His concluding 'nerve of taste indeed!' (ll.29-30) is finely ambiguous. The lingual nerve has proved to be '*entirely* sensory,' that is, entirely to do with physical taste, and nothing to do with that other kind of taste which not least has led poetic tongues to invigorate this passage on a false assumption: 'A nerve of taste [in deed]!' and not, vexingly, a nerve which inspires the abstract 'wagg[ings] of the world'.

Subtly, the narrator has shadowed the chronic conflicts and contrasts between the foundations of science and the foundations of art, of the poet 'ranging within the zodiack of his own wit', as Sir Philip Sidney, a contemporary of Shakespeare, observes in his famous *Apologie for Poetrie*. It is ironic that the gentle ridicule of the scientific approach comes from one of its supposed disciples. But it is gentle ridicule – it is the comic, the humane, glimpsed in this passage, which has the ability to reconcile antagonisms, and explain why it is that the narrator can be at once both 'poet' (of sorts) and medic.

Part III
Question and Answer

In this part we seek to answer the questions which students have most frequently raised in the course of our discussions with them about the principles and practice of literary criticism. These questions have ranged from broad theoretical concerns to matters of detail. It is not always possible to deliver clear-cut answers, since some questions can never be finally resolved. We have tried, however, to be as straightforward as possible in our point of view and as helpful as possible in our advice. Our aim is to respond to the issues involved in a way which will help you to arrive at your own well-founded decisions.

(i) Does analysis of a text risk distorting the author's intentions by reading too much into it?

This raises two separate theoretical issues which are, nevertheless, related when it comes to the practice of literary criticism. The question of whether a writer's intentions are ever knowable, even to himself or herself, is one which became of particular importance at the time when criticism developed an especially rigorous form of that close scrutiny of texts pioneered by I. A. Richards and his followers (see Part I, section (iii)). These 'new' critics, as they were called, headed by John Crowe Ransom and other American scholars of the 1930s and 1940s, had a strong influence on literary criticism in Britain in the 1950s and 1960s. They argued that all the reader had to go on when interpreting a text was the words on the page. What the author might have meant when he or she wrote those words is something the reader cannot know, just as one person cannot read another's mind. Even if the author were to present a thorough and detailed account of what his or her intentions were at the time of writing, this could not be taken as conclusive. People can be deceived about what they mean, especially if the explanation is retrospective: the mind distorts or forgets very easily. Even if the statement of intention were closer in time to the text itself, its literary expression would be different from what might be discovered in, say, letters or autobiography. In Part I we cited Hamlet's words to his mother, where he makes a distinction between his mourning clothes and his inner feelings: 'I have that within which passes show:/These but the trappings and the suits of woe'. But, as we stressed, that which is 'within' can only be revealed by that which is 'without'. All Hamlet's mother, and the audience or readers, have to guide their understanding of him and his emotions is what can be heard and what can be seen, his words and his clothes.

Some of the critical methods we discussed in Part I do rely on the assumption that the meaning of a text can be related to intention. That form of ideological theory which allows the individual writer the capacity to engage critically with the values of his or her society would be one obvious example. The conflicting view that texts simply reveal the ideological bases of a culture, however, sees intentionality as a false construction of the bourgeois emphasis upon individuality. The liberal-humanist, who belongs to the tradition attacked by such a form of Marxist thought, naturally tends to accord freedom of intention to the writer. But whether the ability to relate text to intention leads to an identification between text and intention remains a debatable matter. Any conclusion, then, like 'therefore the author has realized his (or her) intentions . . .' is neither verifiable nor a valid statement of approval.

For the practical purpose of critical analysis, where we may have very little information about the author, or none at all, it is the other element of the question which is more pressing. Is there a danger that our analysis will become more and more intricate, more and more strained, and less and less in touch with the text itself, as we look for ways to impress an examiner? Will this result in a good mark but a mangled text? Should not a poem or novel yield its pleasures and meaning directly, without any need for the elaborate paraphernalia of criticism? Are not books, indeed, simply entertainment, so that the hard work of analysis is actually counter to their very nature?

A sense of proportion is important here. Although some forms of modern theory (as outlined in Part I, section (iii)) argue that any reading of a text, however apparently fanciful, is as justified as any other, the view which underlies the exercise in which we are engaged is the common-sense one that readings have to be reasonably and convincingly argued. That is what distinguishes perceptive intelligence from flashy cleverness. The problem of how such a reasonable interpretation can be achieved can only be solved by practice, by the challenge of explaining in speech or writing how it is that we arrive at a view and then opening our argument to the criticism of others. Hence exposure to discussion-group work can often be a good test of how valid our ideas are: students are usually the most searching audience for their fellow-students. And we all know when our own writing does not even convince ourselves.

The extreme logic of the position implied in the question is simply untenable. To say that a text must make its effect immediately, without any need for thinking about it, is to make a proposition which, in any other sphere of learning, would be universally derided. Apply the idea to the study of mathematics, the sciences or history and the point will be evident. Such a proposition posits that language, which all experience shows to be a complex and ambiguous medium, is self-explanatory and simple in effect. It is to claim an ideal world in which truth strikes us with immediate conviction, as it does for the horses in the fourth book of Swift's *Gulliver's Travels*. In the world of humans, for better or worse, language is the medium of continuing debate.

(ii) How is it possible both to avoid a special 'Eng. Lit.' jargon and yet at the same time use technical terms to advantage?

Quality of thought depends largely upon the clarity and accuracy of the language in which it is expressed. Any confusion in the use of language muddles our account of a text (or, indeed, of anything else on which we are commenting). The proper purpose of technical terms is to help the process of analysing a piece of writing concisely and exactly.

There are different kinds of terms which will be appropriate in different contexts. There are terms which define the *genre* of a piece ('pastoral', 'tragedy', etc.), terms which describe methods of expression ('metaphor', 'irony', etc.), and terms which specify the technical means employed ('syntax', 'iambic pentameter', etc.). Some of these terms are themselves difficult to define – the nature of tragedy, for example, has been, and will continue to be, long and loudly argued over – but they all do provide a language in which discussion can be efficiently conducted. It is much easier to say that a line of poetry is an iambic pentameter than to say that it contains five stressed syllables and five unstressed syllables, the stressed and unstressed syllables alternating, with the stressed following the unstressed. It is also easier to discuss the notion that a word might have both an ostensible meaning and another, hidden, meaning (which is the opposite of the first and which seems to be that which is really meant) if we know how to use the word 'irony'. If we do, then we can more surely avoid the loose and inaccurate usage of such terms which it is all too easy to slip into. An ability to use them precisely provides a vocabulary of literary criticism as useful for us as a knowledge of scientific terms is for the efficient pursuit of scientific enquiry.

There are, however, two important qualifications to be made. The first we have touched on in Part I, section (iv): it is essential that terms are only employed if you are quite clear about their meaning. While this is, in some cases, simply a matter of careful and thorough learning, in others only extensive experience and reading can lead to a measure of confidence. If *King Lear* is the only 'tragedy' that you have read, how justified are you in freely using the term? Our central point that the more you read the more critically aware you become is again the relevant one.

Secondly, technical terms are not an end in themselves. If we use them as though they were ('This poems consists of three stanzas of iambic pentameters rhyming a b a b c c' – end of analysis), then we are just employing 'Eng. Lit.' terms which do not communicate anything meaningful about the passage. Technical terms have decayed into jargon. As we have emphasized throughout, the important focus of critical attention is upon how a writer uses the tools of the trade to create meaning. The choice of which words to rhyme in an a b a b c c pattern, the decision to alter the basic rhythm of a poem at a significant word, so making the metre falling (trochaic) rather than rising (iambic); the use of irony to undermine an attitude in order to expose its inadequacy – these are the ways in which technique creates meaning. Thus it is a writer's artistry which initially demands our observation and response if we are to perceive and understand meaning. A knowledge of technical terms provides us with a vocabulary with which we can develop this task of comprehension.

(iii) If judgements are finally subjective, will an examiner who dis-agrees with a point of view expressed by a candidate mark the answer harshly?

As we noted in Part I, the problem of objectivity of judgement is a vexed one. The notion of there being a stable interpretation of a text has come in for increasingly severe scrutiny. Indeed, it is not merely recent theory which has been sceptical. Wiser opponents of the idea that all judgements are subjective have always been guarded in their definition of 'objectivity'. For Samuel Johnson in the eighteenth cen-tury, for example, critical reputations could only, if at all, derive from the agreed experience of a large variety and number of readers over many years. Since several generations have found *Paradise Lost* to be a powerful and stimulating epic, then, should I find it weak and tedious I ought perhaps to reflect that the fault may lie in me rather than in *Paradise Lost*. Such a conclusion is not absolutely obligatory; but it is, at least, probable.

Deconstructive readings (discussed in Part I, section (iii)) make the impossibility of an objective view of a text their starting-point: lan-guage, stripped of any grounding in reality, can only be an infinite series of signifiers with infinite resonance. One logical – and perhaps attractive – result of this approach is that the whole idea of examining literature is nonsense, because there is no standard against which an individual's response or the text itself can be judged.

You can be reassured, however, that examiners are aware of all problems of subjectivity. They are not looking for a series of 'right' answers; but, on the other hand, they are there to evaluate the quality of whatever answers you present. Of its very nature, evaluation may involve some estimation of right and wrong. Communication depends for its very existence on a common assumption of definitions of language. So, if a candidate discusses the opening line of T. S. Eliot's *The Waste Land* ('April is the cruellest month . . .') in terms of its magnificent evocation of autumnal mellowness, an examiner will feel perfectly justified in being less than generous in marking (while probably wondering if the library has confused its cataloguing of Eliot and Keats). Yet that same examiner will not mark essays on *The Waste Land* with a totally fixed view of, say, Eliot's choice of allusions to myth and literature, ticking or crossing according to whether or not the candidate's interpretation coincides with his or hers. This is obviously the case with a notoriously difficult text like *The Waste Land*, but the lesson holds good in general terms: we can distinguish between elements of a text which cannot reasonably admit of major disagreement and others which are properly open to informed debate. The key rule to remember is that conclusions must be apportioned to the evidence adduced.

Human beings are judgemental in tendency: even the most convinced deconstructionists will argue for their view, if only in defence of their theory. We judge critics according to their ability to convince us by marshalling evidence, arguing their points and drawing our attention not only to what we have seen but also to what we have overlooked. Your tutor or examiner is in precisely this situation when marking your work. It is as true of critical as of creative writing that what is said cannot be separated from the way in which it is said. An examiner will respond positively to analyses which are well stated and thoroughly argued, and negatively to a tissue of undefended and unexplained assertions. In an imperfect world, this is the best we can expect.

(iv) When discussing passages, should we stick entirely to what is on the page, or should we bring in outside material?

The centre of the exercise is the passage itself, and this must therefore be throughout the focus of an answer. Nevertheless, texts are not read in a vacuum: a reader's knowledge of other books, as well as his or her experience in general, will inevitably inform a response to a text. The more we read, the wider and deeper our literary awareness becomes, the more likely we are to see relationships between a new text and what we have read. These relationships can be productive, providing helpful points of comparison. Thus, for example, a reader with a good knowledge of how comic conventions of disguise operate in drama of the period will be well placed to perceive the implications we discuss in our analysis of passage (iii). Similarities and dissimilarities can help to clarify the way in which an idea is being treated. Historical awareness, in the case of our comparative accounts of John Hampden (passage (iv)), provides a context which will, at the very least, make the subject-matter of a passage more familiar.

If such knowledge can be applied constructively to an analysis, then it can legitimately be used. If a symbolic passage from a Hardy novel reminds us of a comparable passage from another Hardy novel, then a good point could be made. If, say, the excerpt cited is that description in *Tess of the D'Urbervilles* of light from a train momentarily picking out the motionless figure of Tess (chapter 30), then knowledge of the significance of railways in marking the break-up of Wessex society in *Jude the Obscure* would suggest a recurrent theme in the novels and reinforce an interpretation of the *Tess* passage in similar terms.

But an examiner will not be expecting such complementary knowledge, and an answer without it will not be penalized. An ability to use this knowledge, however, will indicate a student's ability to focus his or her range of reading on the question in hand. The essential qualification is that information must be relevant to the text under discussion: the point must be made out of the example rather than arbitrarily imposed upon it. No benefit will be gained from self-evidently forced analogies which vainly seek to impress a gullible examiner. Proportion, too, is important: all additional material must be kept strictly subservient to the main aim of the exercise, that of presenting a sensitive analysis of the passage specified.

(v) How far should we be guided by typography (capitals, italics, punctuation, spelling, etc.) when looking at a text?

Interpretation of typography is a vexed question in literary studies. In texts of earlier periods, decisions about capital letters, spelling and punctuation would have been taken by the printer, often with no reference at all to the author. Convention, too, would have operated in such typographical matters as giving nouns initial capital letters, a practice retained in modern German. It is thus very dangerous to interpret typographical features too definitely. This can also apply to modern texts: there is a salutary story of a literary critic who wrote in praise of the perfect placing of a comma in a line of a poem, only to discover afterwards that the said comma was a misprint. Even in the case of punctuation which is definitely not a misprint, modern editors will often disagree about its status, some regarding it as an essential part of a text and others as merely accidental.

The practice in many editions of older works – the Arden edition of the plays of Shakespeare is a well-known instance – is to modernize spelling and regularize punctuation. We have chosen to follow this procedure in printing our examples. However, syllabuses with their range of set texts do, at least implicitly, take account of historical period. Some critics would argue that texts can only be properly discussed if set within their historical context. There is advantage to be gained by demonstrating an awareness of period, both as a guide to interpretation and as a further indication of literary sophistication. Even in modernized texts, language or syntax may provide significant clues: the archaic word 'sirrah' in passage (iii), for example, suggests an approximate date which is relevant to the social attitudes implied. More advanced students of English will certainly encounter these concerns which are of great importance for the practice of secure and confident criticism, as well as for a consideration of the nature and problems involved in editorship.

It is sufficient, though, for our present purposes to note that a text as it appears on an examination paper can be taken as definitive for the purposes of the exercise. It is, therefore, perfectly proper to interpret italicization or capitalization as an indication of emphasis, and to make observations from details of punctuation. Punctuation can, indeed, be a crucial factor in determining meaning, as our analysis of passage (v) has especially demonstrated. Everything on the page is part of the meaning.

Consequently, it is important that you should be conscious of the differing usages and placing of commas, colons, semi-colons and so on. Just as an acquaintance with literary terms assists greatly in providing an exact and expressive vocabulary for criticism (see question (ii)), so a knowledge of how precisely punctuation supports and creates meaning will help to sharpen a reading of a text. It will also, of course, be invaluable in developing your own writing skills.

(vi) What is the distinction between such terms as 'mood' and 'atmosphere'?

The specific answer here is that 'mood' refers to people and 'atmosphere' to the environment. The etymological derivation of 'mood' is from words meaning 'mind', 'thought': hence the term can be used to indicate a person's frame of mind or state of feelings. We might, then, discuss how a novelist presents the mood of a character. The derivation of 'atmosphere' is from astronomical terms (from Greek words meaning 'vapour' and 'ball' or 'sphere'), and refers literally to the gases surrounding a planet. By extension, the word can be used of any surroundings, including the environment of landscape or townscape. We can thus speak of how Hardy creates the atmosphere of Egdon Heath as a setting for his characters in *The Return of the Native*. How these characters respond (or how a reader responds) will be in terms of 'mood'. The literary usage of both these terms illustrates how figurative meanings develop from literal meanings. Sometimes the figurative meaning is so frequently used that we can mistake it for the literal.

Usage becomes so well tried that it is even difficult to distinguish between the two. For example, what is the status of the word 'pouring' in the all-too-familiar observation 'it's pouring with rain'?

More generally, this question raises the issue of how we employ descriptive terms when analysing a piece of writing. There are two reasons why we must be wary in our use of them. First, it is so easy to employ them loosely. Thus critics may talk glibly of the 'mood' of a work of art, and be unaware that they are confusing the way in which objects are painted with their effects on an observer. This distinction needs to be kept in mind all the more carefully when analysing a descriptive passage in literature. As we pointed out in our answer to question (ii), as clear and exact a use of language as possible is essential to ensure a clear and exact expression of our ideas. The second cause for concern is that descriptive words can become a substitute for real thinking, rather than the expression of real thinking. Because 'mood' and 'atmosphere' and their like are metaphors when applied to language, they can easily be used evasively. To describe an image as 'atmospheric' – like describing it as 'beautiful' or 'effective' – does not mean anything. It is how the 'atmosphere' is created and what, precisely, that 'atmosphere' is which require our exploration.

So, if we are tempted, when confronted by a piece of descriptive writing, to say something like, 'The mood of the scene is very effective', we should recall that our own language, in this or any other instance, must be both accurate and meaningful. An endeavour to investigate fully the kinds of expression used by the author which compose the description will result in a much greater comprehension of how a piece of writing works.

(vii) How do you deal with what you suspect to be a poor piece of writing?

The method of literary criticism is the same whatever the text being studied. Your suspicions about the quality of the writing should, therefore, in no way alter your basic approach to it.

Qualitative judgements are, in any case, highly contentious: what a person likes or dislikes may say as much about the person as about the text. Nevertheless, we all inevitably have our ideas of what constitutes good or bad writing; and there is no reason why expressions of approval or disapproval should not play a part in our analysis. Indeed, it is questionable whether we could avoid them even if we wished to. The issue is associated with that of objectivity and subjectivity (see question (iii)).

We should, however, be careful about rushing into judgements and about intemperate expression of them. If a question invites or demands evaluation, it is essential that we argue a case rather than simply proffer unsubstantiated opinions. We should give due attention to contrary evidence, not merely employ that which supports our prejudice. The test of our literary sensitivity lies in the capacity to assess and express the reasons for a decision rather than in the decision itself. Thus it is as important to establish an analytic language for ineffectiveness as it is to establish one for effectiveness. The clearest way to do this is to have in mind a yardstick by which we can measure how far our example falls short of the ideal. The ineffectiveness of an image can only be determined in relation to what the effect might have been. When the Victorian poet Swinburne describes the gradual awakening of nature in spring in terms of 'lisp of leaves and ripple of rain', we might ask ourselves whether 'lisp' (that is, substituting 'th' for a sibilant in speech) is an appropriate word for the sound of leaves moving in a breeze, and whether it is a characteristic unique to breezes at that time of year. In order to test this, we could substitute other words we might think of as appropriate ('rustle'?), and then judge whether 'lisp' is less effective (inaccurate? if so, why?) or more effective (more arresting in attributing a human sound to nature?). Whatever our conclusion, we shall have established a line of argument by comparison which will serve as the basis for its support.

(viii) If posed a question in 'either/or' form, do we have to make a definite decision one way or the other?

Literature is not necessarily divided into the right and the wrong, the good and the bad. It plays off a series of possibilities, of which one, some, or even all may be appropriate at the same time. So a question in a format which invites choice between two alternatives may legitimately receive a qualified, rather than forthright, answer. A comparison between two texts may reveal so many different qualities, attitudes and styles that points of similarity cannot be defined. Texts are not always capable of being reduced to common factors.

A style which we find unattractive may nonetheless prove appropriate to its own subject-matter. A text which takes a definite attitude to its subject-matter may well evoke contrary responses in its readers. Equally, a text which is open-ended can still betray readers into airing their prejudices. This is particularly so if the subject is an inherently contentious one (politics, war, religion). This awareness should stop us making simple choices. Arguments for or against should be part of a sophisticated reply to an either/or question. This need not prevent your offering a final opinion if this is required, but a discriminating answer demonstrates insight, not lack of conviction.

A tendency which we have found recurrent in students' discussions seems related to this kind of question. We have often been asked to help by providing clear, definite answers to questions like 'whose side is the playwright on?', 'who is the hero of this novel?', 'is this play a tragedy or a history?'. But a playwright might be dramatizing a conflict, in which both sides are seen to display virtues and vices; a novelist might present both admirable and unattractive aspects of a character without taking sides for or against; a work of art can operate in such a way as to be inconclusive. Rather than this being a source of worry, it should reassure you that literature does not possess answers to problems which our experience of life cannot resolve. A not insubstantial part of literature's fascination lies in its ability to present us at each reading with new or revised insights to measure against those gained from previous readings.

(ix) **In answering 'compare and contrast' questions, which method is the better: (a) to take the texts separately and conclude by noting factors of comparison and contrast, or (b) to take individual points in turn, and refer to them in both passages?**

There is no definitive method of structuring an answer which will apply equally to all questions. The structure of an analysis will derive from a suitable ordering of the points which are most significant in the text. Nevertheless, exercises which demand that two or more passages are compared and contrasted do present particular structural problems.

Both methods have their advantages and disadvantages. The first is the easier to put into practice, and the one which, as long as we keep our eye on the clock, more readily ensures that equal time is spent on each of the passages. Its danger, though, is that it can easily lapse into separate, distinct analyses followed by a perfunctory attempt to note a few brief points of comparison and contrast. Discussing each passage in turn may make you forget what the purpose of the exercise is. Any text will inevitably contain elements worthy of observation which do not fit into a sensible comparative study (there being a limit to how far complete differences can be meaningfully discussed as contrasts). Concentration upon one text at a time may lead you to discuss material which is not strictly relevant. It is thus important, if pursuing this method, to think carefully about points of comparison first, so that the separate analyses will focus on ideas which the conclusion can take up with respect to both or all the texts. If this method is adopted, it is as well to make an occasional glance back and forth, so that the conclusion is not set the task of making all the points of comparison. That conclusion must form a major section of the whole answer, rather than be tacked unconvincingly on the end.

Method (b) has the crucial advantage of preventing you from running away with one text by keeping the aim of the exercise continually before you. Its problems are that it can seem, initially at least, more difficult to organize, and that the overall shape and argument of the passages can become lost in a discussion of a series of details. These, however, are not insuperable: practice will both speed up the process of organizing an answer, and ensure that you acquire the habit of attending to the structure of an individual passage as well as to details within it. It may be helpful to range the points for discussion in a list (e.g. 'language and other points of style', 'development of argument', 'narrative method', 'attitude of writer to subject-matter', etc.) in order that no important area is omitted.

When most fully achieved, the second method is the more satisfactory, because the process of comparison is more fully integrated into the answer than is the case with the alternative method. In writing our examples of 'comparison and contrast' in this book, we have deliberately varied the methods used so that you can judge for yourself the relative effectiveness of them.

(x) When answering 'compare and contrast' questions, what points of comparison (stylistic, thematic?) should we be looking for?

Unless a question directs you to specific areas for discussion, assume that all aspects of the passage should be referred to. The obvious qualification is that a particular set of passages may focus on a shared topic, which therefore provides your essay with its emphasis: a series of passages, for example, describing people's experiences of different landscapes will probably invite the varying attitudes they adopt to be the central point of comparison.

However, even when a very clear theme for comparison is suggested, it is important to remember that all elements of a text are interrelated: style and content are ultimately indivisible, the latter being shaped and created by the former. So, if we were discussing two poems about experiences in war, we would want to observe how the abstract language of such lines as 'I have a rendezvous with Death/ When Spring brings back blue days and fair' (Alan Seeger, 'Rendezvous') embodies a very different attitude from that implied in lines like 'A man's brains splattered on/A stretcher-bearer's face' (Isaac Rosenberg, 'Dead Man's Dump'). As we saw in our comparison of accounts of John Hampden (passage (iv)), it is choice of language, rhetorical structures, and other stylistic features which actually form the meaning. These, then, are our clues to the attitudes each writer is taking towards what may be exactly the same subject. Even when one element may appear dominant, it is important to observe how all are connected. The most perceptive analysis will link the various aspects of texts.

(xi) Since the amount of time available in an examination is very limited, how can we try to speed up the process of reading, assessing and writing about a text?

The speed which examinations impose upon the reading process is at odds with the way in which literary sensitivity is formed by our freedom to read and develop at our own pace.

Our response should, however, not be simply negative. The same problems exist for everyone taking the exam, and, as in all tasks of life, it is up to us to adapt efficiently to the conditions we meet. Since time is crucial in examinations, it is important to use it as productively as possible. The first rule is to divide your time equally between all parts of an examination paper in order to avoid unfinished or hastily completed scripts. As we stressed in Part I, no matter how well you perform on two thirds of a paper, your maximum marks remain two thirds of the total. The same principle applies to apportioning time within answers. In addition, good results will only be achieved if time is carefully divided between reading and writing. The answer you produce depends initially upon the intensity and quality of your reading; and we consequently have recommended in Part I, section (iv) that a passage is read attentively at least three times before an answer is attempted.

But preparation does not begin in the exam room. The quality of your reading there derives from the extent of your experience of reading texts alertly and intelligently elsewhere. The process of understanding what is going on should be at the heart of all our reading. The most valuable advice that we can repeat in this final answer is that extensive reading, with a constant alertness to the significance of language, is the finest preparation for all literary criticism. This is true of language in any circumstances: for example we can learn by asking ourselves what is meant – or not meant – by an advertisement which boasts of a 'unique offer'. This experience and attentiveness produce sharper and quicker perceptions.

While reading and re-reading the passage before you, make rapid notes of outstanding features of language, style and content, so that you build up a profile of the text which can then be shaped into a coherent analysis. It may be that some features initially noted do not lead anywhere in terms of the final analysis, and can later be discarded. For example, an image in one line of a poem may not seem to shed any light upon the rest of it; whereas another image may at once suggest a connection with the poem's theme. It is by rapidly noting these features that distinctions can be spotted, and decisions about what to include and exclude be taken as quickly as possible.

Try, finally, to give some shape to your answer. Its structure will be influenced by decisions made at the reading stage, so that no generalizations can be made about organization. Once again, practice is the route to speed and success.

Glossary

As we said earlier, this list is by no means exhaustive. Where necessary we explained terms as we went along. Here you will find brief information about other terms we have used.

alliteration   The repetition of an initial letter or letters for the sake of emphasis.

antithesis   Constrasting ideas by balancing words of opposite meaning.

ballad   A poem that tells a story in simple rhymed language. The story is conveyed through dialogue and action, and the themes are often tragic. The literary ballad derives its form and content from folk traditions.

blank verse   A distinctive poetic form of the English language, consisting of unrhymed lines of ten syllables where the basic pattern is five iambic feet – the iambic pentameter.

caesura   A pause or break in a line of poetry.

canon   The works whose excellence has been established over the years by common consensus.

couplet   Two successive lines of verse which rhyme.

elegy   A poem where the poet's contemplation is prompted by a particular death, or death in general.

epigram   A form of writing which condenses its material into brief statement. In poetry the epigram often takes the form of a couplet.

epitaph   Literary writing suitable for a memorial or a gravestone, although it may not actually appear on either.

foot   A group of syllables forming a measurable metrical unit.

free verse   A form of poetry with no regular metre or line length which treats rhyme, if it occurs, with a similar freedom. The mood is created through the irregular rhythmic recurrence of stressed and unstressed syllables – the

111

heightened effects of natural speech patterns – rather than through the formal patterns of poetry.

genre
The type, or class, to which a work belongs – for example: tragedy, comedy, and so on. From earliest times there were thought to be rules of composition appropriate to each genre, but they have been less strictly adhered to in later ages.

iamb
A metrical foot consisting of one unstressed syllable followed by a stressed one. The iambic measure is thought to be particularly agreeable to the English voice and ear, and the majority of English poetry consists of lines made up of iambic feet.

imagery
The writer's use of language to convey images of objects, actions, or states of mind and feelings to the mind of the reader.

irony
Verbal irony occurs when one meaning is stated yet the reader detects that a different, usually opposite, meaning is intended. Dramatic irony occurs when the audience knows more than a character whose reactions are contrary to what they might be had he or she fuller information.

lament
A type of poetry expressing profound sorrow, regret, or concern for a loss.

melodrama
A sensational and exaggeratedly emotional form of drama where events are contrived to license effects, or effects are far in excess of the events which are made to cause them. The term is generally used to describe anything which is overcharged.

metaphor
The expression of one thing in terms of another. A comparison is usually implied rather than stated, so that the reader might judge the aptness of choice, the imaginative power that the writer has achieved in creating the connection.

metre
The recurrence of a rhythmic pattern within a line and corresponding lines of poetry. The type of metre will be determined by the pattern of the stressed and unstressed syllables within the feet which make up the line.

monologue
Poetry or prose where one person speaks alone, with or without an audience.

oxymoron
The combination of two apparently contradictory elements for emphasis or striking effect: Milton's 'darkness visible', for example.

paradox
An observation which appears self-contradictory, but whose truth is emphasized on closer inspection.

pastoral
Writing which treats of rural life, usually in a stylized manner.

pentameter   A line of five feet – in English poetry usually found as five iambic feet making ten syllables in all.

point of view   The position in which the narrator stands in relation to the story; the standpoint from which events are narrated. More often met with in prose criticism than poetry criticism, it is nonetheless relevant to both.

quatrain   A grouping of four lines, rhymed or unrhymed.

rhetoric   Rhetoric is the art of persuasion, and more particularly defined as the forms and ornaments of language which add eloquence and effect to both speech and writing. The term is used loosely to describe elaborate expression.

simile   A comparison of one thing with another where, unlike metaphor, the connection is explicitly indicated by the use of the word 'like' or 'as'.

sonnet   A fourteen-line poem in iambic pentameters whose close argument is aided by a variety of rhyme schemes. In English poetry the commonest forms of sonnet comprise three quatrains and a concluding couplet (as used by Shakespeare), or a division into eight lines (the octave) and a following six (the sestet).

stanza   A sequence of lines arranged in a definite pattern, which is repeated throughout a work. More generally, a group of lines of poetry.

stress   The vocal emphasis given to some syllables of words, as opposed to unstressed ones, as part of the metrical pattern of poetry. The sign for a stressed syllable is '/', an unstressed one '⌣'. Regular combinations of stressed and unstressed syllables are measured in feet which characterize the metre.

symbol   An image which suggests or evokes an idea or conception. A manner of representation in which what is given (usually something material or concrete) suggests, through association, something more, or beyond (usually something immaterial or abstract).

tautology   The repetition of the same thing or idea in different words.

tone   Tone is difficult to pin down because it arises from complex reactions. It is best thought of as the general impression a reader feels that a text, or any part of a text, conveys.

trochee   A metrical foot consisting of one stressed syllable followed by an unstressed one. The trochaic foot is usually encountered as a contrast within an iambic line.

Sources of examples

i Margaret Drabble (1939–), *The Millstone*, 1965.

ii Thomas Hardy (1840–1928), 'A Woman's Fancy', from the volume *Late Lyrics and Earlier*, 1922.

iii William Shakespeare (1564–1616), *The Taming of the Shrew*, 1593–94, Induction, ii, 105–38.

iv A. David Hume (1711–76), *History of England*, 1754–61, ch. 56.
   B. Thomas Babington, Lord Macaulay (1800–59), 'Review of Lord Nugent's *Memorials of Hampden*', 1831.

v Robert Browning (1812–89), 'Inapprehensiveness', from the *Asolando* volume, 1889.

vi Katherine Mansfield (1888–1923), 'The Garden Party', from a collection of short stories of the same title, 1922.

vii A. Mary Shelley (1797–1851), *Frankenstein*, 1818, ch. 9.
   B. George Gordon, Lord Byron (1788–1824), from his *Journals*, 23 September 1816.

viii A. Arthur Symons (1865–1945), 'The Street-Singer', from the volume *Days and Nights*, 1889.
   B. D. H. Lawrence (1885–1930), 'After the Opera', first published in the volume *Bay*, 1919.

ix John Locke (1632–1704), from *An Essay Concerning Human Understanding*, Book I, ch. 1.

x Harold Pinter (1930–), *The Caretaker*, 1960, I, 1–36.

xi A. George Herbert (1593–1633), 'Denial', from *The Temple*, 1633.
   B. Christina Rossetti (1830–94), 'A Better Resurrection', from 'Devotional Poems' in the *Poetical Works*, poem dated 30 June 1857.

xii Arnold Bennett (1867–1931), *Hilda Lessways*, 1911, Book IV, ch. 2.

xiii Charlotte Smith (1748–1806), from *Elegiac Sonnets*, 5th edition, 1789.

xiv A. Charles Dickens (1812–70), *Hard Times*, 1854, Book I. ch. 5.
   B. Walter Greenwood (1903–74), *Love on the Dole*, 1933, Part I, ch. 3.

xv A. Edward Thomas (1878–1917), 'In Memoriam (Easter 1915)', collected in *Poems*, 1917.

B. Siegfried Sassoon (1886–1967), *Siegfried's Journey*, 1945, ch. 5.

xvi William Wordsworth (1770–1850), from *The Excursion* (Book IV, 847–87).

xvii W. M. Thackeray (1811–63), letter to Frederick Gale, 23 Aug. 1851, from Gordon N. Ray, ed., *The Letters and Private Papers of William Makepeace Thackeray*, 1945, 4 vols., II, 798–99.

xviii A. W. H. Auden (1907–73), from *Letter to Lord Byron*, 1937.

B. Iris Murdoch (1919–), *A Word Child*, 1975.

xix Virginia Woolf (1882–1941), ' "Jane Eyre" and "Wuthering Heights" ', from a collection of essays called *The Common Reader*, 1925.

xx Walt Whitman (1819–92), Section 21, 'Song of Myself', from *Leaves of Grass*, first published 1855 and revised up to 1892.

xxi Oliver St John Gogarty (1878–1957), *Tumbling in the Hay*, first published 1939, ch. II, 'In College Park'.

Index

116